Parenting Toddlers

Parenting Made Easy, Enhance Your Family Life
and Learn How to Balance Discipline

(How to Build Children's Confidence and
Emotional Maturity)

Richard Paxton

Published by Rob Miles

© **Richard Paxton**

All Rights Reserved

Parenting Toddlers: Parenting Made Easy, Enhance Your Family Life and Learn How to Balance Discipline (How to Build Children's Confidence and Emotional Maturity)

ISBN 9781990084393

All rights reserved. No part of this guide may be reproduced in any form without permission in writing from the publisher except in the case of brief quotations embodied in critical articles or reviews.

Legal & Disclaimer

The information contained in this book is not designed to replace or take the place of any form of medicine or professional medical advice. The information in this book has been provided for educational and entertainment purposes only.

The information contained in this book has been compiled from sources deemed reliable, and it is accurate to the best of the Author's knowledge; however, the Author cannot guarantee its accuracy and validity and cannot be held liable for any errors or omissions. Changes are periodically made to this book. You must consult your doctor or get professional medical advice before using any of the suggested remedies, techniques, or information in this book.

Upon using the information contained in this book, you agree to hold harmless the Author from and against any damages, costs, and expenses, including any legal fees potentially resulting from the application of any of the information provided by this guide. This disclaimer applies to any damages or injury caused by the use and application, whether directly or indirectly, of any advice or information presented, whether for breach of contract, tort, negligence, personal injury, criminal intent, or under any other cause of action.

You agree to accept all risks of using the information presented inside this book. You need to consult a professional medical practitioner in order to ensure you are both able and healthy enough to participate in this program.

Table of Contents

INTRODUCTION 1

CHAPTER 1: UNDERSTANDING CHILDREN'S MOTIVES 13

CHAPTER 2: GOOD PARENTING SKILLS 18

CHAPTER 3: YOU SURVIVED THE EARLY YEARS... 23

CHAPTER 4: STARTING AN ALLOWANCE 29

CHAPTER 5: BEING MATURE DURING AND AFTER A DIVORCE 35

CHAPTER 6: WHY FAMILY TIME MATTERS 41

CHAPTER 7: STEP DAD STRATEGIES TO BUILD BETTER BLENDED FAMILIES 44

CHAPTER 8: TIPS FOR BUILDING CHARACTER 47

CHAPTER 9: WATCH YOUR TIME FILLERS 55

CHAPTER 10: AGES AND STAGES 62

CHAPTER 11: MARRIAGE – KIDS – DIVORCE 67

CHAPTER 12: STARTING EVERY DAY WITH A HEALTHY BREAKFAST IN A FAST-PACED WORLD 74

CHAPTER 13: THE MEANING OF TANTRUM TODDLER 78

CHAPTER 14: HOW TO MENTALLY PREPARE TO DEAL WITH YOUR GROWING TODDLER..............................92

CHAPTER 15: TONE AND BODY LANGUAGE 99

CHAPTER 16: OUR EVER CHANGING ROLE IN HOW TO BE A GOOD PARENT 108

CHAPTER 17: HELPING YOUR CHILD REALIZE HIS OR HER TALENTS.. 111

CHAPTER 18: ENCOURAGE THEIR INTERESTS................. 121

CHAPTER 19: RELEVANCE OF DIVORCE TO CHILDREN..... 127

CHAPTER 20: ADOLESCENT PROBLEMS.......................... 134

CHAPTER 21: CHANGES THAT OCCUR AS YOUR TEEN GROWS UP 139

CHAPTER 22: GETTING YOURSELF AND YOUR CHILD READY FOR CHANGES 143

CHAPTER 23: TANTRUM MANAGEMENT TECHNIQUES.. 149

CHAPTER 24: THE AFFECTS FOR PARENTS...................... 154

CHAPTER 25: HOW TO BE IN THE DATING GAME AS A SINGLE PARENT 158

CHAPTER 26: COMMUNICATION WITH YOUR CHILD 171

CONCLUSION... 177

Introduction

What is a parent? The answer to this question will probably include, either implicitly or explicitly, specific assumptions, based on the rights and duties of parents. Biological motherhood and fatherhood are often considered synonymous. But of course, they are adoptive parents assuming the role of parents. It's a common sense not only opening a review of the possible links between biology and parenting, but also other aspects such as the role of consent in acquiring the rights and obligations of parenting, which then takes a series of other issues that are not important, but have a theoretically meaningful existence (Dcss.smcgov.org, n.d.). What this means for a parent to have rights as a parent? Why to think there are these rights? What are the duties of parents toward their children? What is the role of the State, as appropriate, regarding the relationship between parents and children? These questions are crucial for understanding the political, personal, social, and moral dimensions of the parents-children relationship.

Definition of a good person can vary depending on the fact that who is being asked. Defining a good parent is however same as trying to define a good person. However, some generalizations are there that are common of a good parent. Parents should have a basic love of really caring about their children. This involves paying attention and showing affection to the child. A good family atmosphere should be created and maintained by parents. . "A good parent should also be a good person". They should possess the capital and resources to support the child as their birth is only a smaller part of all this. General characteristics of understanding, responsibility, patience, and care should be possessed by them. A decent parent is somebody who can give love, the necessities of life for themselves and their children.

If children are not loved by their parent then there is no hope for them to be good parents. "Love is the quality most essential to create a constructive parent-child relationship. When there is no love presented by parent, it will created problems in the child. A solid foundation of love is very favorable for a good parent, if the parent is not able to express their love, and the child does not know that their parents love them, it is useless" (Hinds et al., 2009). Giving the child enough attention and affection are two good examples showing that how parents can show their love for children.

A crucial role in child development is played by parenting styles. In fact, research has uncovered that parenting styles can impact a youngster's mental, intellectual, and social development, that influences kids both in adulthood and in adolescence years. Children, on these grounds, develop through a series of stimuli, exchange, and interaction which surround them. The way that parents are consistently around the life of a child, will impact him/her either negatively or positively. This report addresses the parenting styles adopted in different countries by parents (Aunola, Stattin, and Nurmi, 2000).

There are four commonly known parenting styles. They include, "authoritative, authoritarian, indulgent, and neglectful parenting". "Authoritative" parenting style is both demanding and responsive. Parents who use this style parents teach their children to be independent and control their actions. "Authoritative" parents teach children to control their feeling and also understand their emotions. Moreover, authoritative parents always need to be mature. Punishments are not arbitrary or violent in this style but they are prevalent. Due to various constraints, this style has the advantage that children respond appropriately (Aunola, Stattin, and Nurmi, 2000).

The next parenting style is "Authoritarian" parenting style. It is both demanding and unresponsive and is also known as strict parenting. The main feature of this style is that children are expected to comply with all rules and respect their parents. This parenting style has minimal open communication between children and parents. Often authoritarian parenting style includes following the rules without a single reason why restrictions and standards are being set. Research shows that parents adopting this style of parenting do not satisfy the emotional needs of the child (Smetana, 1995). Therefore, low social competence is being shown by these children because their parents do not allow them to make decisions of their own.

Third parenting style is indulgent parenting and it is responsive and undemanding. Parents adopting this style are usually lenient and permissive, simply because there are few expectations they have from their children (Rhee, et al., 2006). "Indulgent" parents set very few limits and rules and are normally involved with their children. Children are seen, frequently, as spoiled and rude rose through this style. This is because their parents do not teach them to control their feelings.

Neglectful parenting is the last parenting style. "Unlike the other three, neglectful parenting is neither demanding nor responsive". Rather, parents are totally uninvolved with the youngster's development. "Neglectful" parents are generally insensitive and disregard the emotional needs of their children. Children are often independent and mature in this parenting style; even though they tend to be psychologically resistant to others (Glasgow, et al., 1997). Also, they cannot express their feelings easily. Following figure shows the four parenting styles.

Figure 2: Parenting Styles

It is believed that learning in the early years of a child make a "significant difference" in how they develop and continue to learn in life (Kim, 1999). The role of parents and their impact on the development of child has been examined by the developmental psychologists. However, it is relatively a tough task to develop a cause-and-effect link between brought up and parents behavior and impact of it on child attitude and behavior. This is obvious from the fact that those who children are brought up and developed in same environment sharing a home, may develop different personalities under same circumstances from each other. Based on regular strategies, a parenting style is psychological conception used by parents while raising their child. To raise a child, there are various concepts and theories about perfect and best ways. In raising a child, parenting style plays a crucial role. Four different parenting styles are identified by Baumrind's theory. Different parenting techniques are covered world widely by all these.

Responsibilities of parents start soon after birth and are of much significance, and could have an impact on the life of a child. Parents in most cases, usually, develop their own parenting style based on the fusion of factors such as temperament and other influences, which have been observed in families due to the training and surrounding culture. There is no absolute rule for parents, usually it develops over time children grow and develop personality. The quality of the parents has a profound impact on the development of emotional, intellectual, and social development of the children (Essays, UK. 2013). As parents have done is important to address and improve the effects of children as they progress socially and individually. Child development is affected by several factors, for example, humans and environment are in close contact and interaction. Parental influence is more on the development of a child; positivity and negativity in the attitude and behavior of a child are due to parenting style and development.

It is not an indisputable fact that schools should have classes to teach children to be good parents who in the future would manage the family, including education of children. While this is a good idea to teach children to be good parents like this, but some critics say it's a waste of time to concentrate on academic career rather enabling parents to develop them perfectly.

There are some reasons why people believe the younger generation should learn to be a better parent in a family. Firstly, time management in different aspect in making children effluent and managing expenditures of family by targeting to flourish the name and fame of family. Perfect parent can handle a lot of trouble to keep the family living happily, as a result, parents can make young students as bright, efficient tutors to accelerate socio-economic development and good self-sufficient in practical life. Second, the family is an important part of a large organization that is required to lead the country through innovative and creative ways. Young people who are literate with the idea of being good and educated parents effectively implement the future of family.

Gaining knowledge on how to be a good partner can be very valuable for the young generation and their development. Thirdly, how to judge, how to understand, how to deal with the wide range of problems that occur in life, learners will be able to learn the lesson of being good parents and showing good behavior. A best nation can be produced by good educated parent that will hasten the country's overall development.

Effective parenting has never been so important to the success of family than today. Coming generations would be shaped by proper parenting, and also it will shape the behavior of next generations which will affect the world around them. History has shown that without a proper foundation, parenting has always been tragic and ultimately leads to the state of confusion developing children. Therefore, trying to be a good parent is of much importance in life and is also a challenging task (DeVore and Ginsburg, 2005).

Try to know the healthy methods that are best for upbringing a child may seem time consuming during parenting but it is a rewarding effort. This report addresses parenting in detail and tries to define and evaluate parenting in different aspects. It also addresses the parental rights, responsibilities and obligations. Parenting styles and Diana Baumrind theory is also discussed in detail. Also, the factors that affect the parent-child relationship are discussed.

Chapter 1: Understanding Children's Motives

Naturally, every child is good, and no child is ever born bad or uncontrollable.Parents who have uncontrollable teenagers seem to be more confused as to why their children have behaved in such manner.Instead of digging into the reasons of such behavior, most parents usually blame their children for being so ill mannered and even blame their peers as well as their activities as the causes of such behavior.

Furthermore, most parents often complain that their advice is often being ignored and whatever they do, their children simply seem to not care.Of course, their children often care but they are just too unyielding for the main reason of rebellion.They have their reasons for doing such and those reasons should be what their parents should look into. It is so very easy to get caught up in the moment.

When I say this I mean the child's behavior at that minute, instead of taking a step back and saying to oneself, "why or what is the reason is my child acting this way", instead of saying to yourself "this child needs to stop acting this way, this is the end of it". Instead of getting mad at your child's behavior.

The following are some tips as to how parents can counteract the bad behavior of their children through understanding their motives behind their behavior.

Behavior checking

One of the most common mistakes parents commit while parenting is on the way they handle themselves on the situation with their children.Once the behavior of the children seemed to differ from how they were before, primarily is to check one's own behavior.Parents must try answering these questions to clear their minds and focus more on what they need to do.

Have I been busy with other things lately?

Have I helped my children in making their assignments?

Have I deeply listen to them when they call my attention?

How much of my time has been alloted for my kids each day?

Have I been difficult or rather harsh to my children too?

The list of questions could go on.The parents alone could answer these questions, being defensive could create more problems, so parents should be honest with themselves.Most often, children became more difficult to handle when they think that their parents have been too unfair in their treatment to them.Rebellion is their way of retaliating to their parents and they could do so by being difficult to handle, stubborn, and unruly.

Be a keen observer

Parents most often observe their kids in such a wrong way because they always look for the negative things and failed to praise the positive ones.When they observe something that they do not like, they always reprimand their kids in such a manner that could hurt the feelings of their children.This is definitely wrong; parents need to analyze what made their children act in such manner.By observing their children's behavior keenly doesn't mean that they could be too critical too about it.Parents must observe, be more casual, and confront their kids in such a right timing and in a right way.

Understand their motives

Parents could not always get why their children become too difficult to handle and this is because they never know what their motives are for such behavior.Once they know the reasons behind their children's behavior for sure they will no longer be too hard on them too.Children's motives for being difficult could always involve ways that for them could just be for fun, they want to get the kind of attention they want, and one major reason could be that they plainly want to retaliate to their parents.Parents could always have some alternative courses of action on what they need to do for each of this reason only if they know it.Parents could have a clear understanding to why their children have acted in such ways if they would only be open-minded and observe keenly their children's activities.

Chapter 2: Good parenting skills

Good parenting helps foster empathy, honesty, self-reliance, self-control, kindness, cooperation and cheerfulness. It also promotes intellectual curiosity, motivation and a desire to achieve. It prevents children from developing anxiety, depression, eating disorders and anti-social behavior.

Too many parents base their action on their own gut reaction. Some use hitting as a form of discipline and others use time-out. Many parents use the same tactics their own parents used and a lot of times that meant using really harsh discipline.

The relationship between a parent and their child will be reflected in the child's action — including child behavior problems. If you don't have a good relationship with your child, they will not listen to you.

Here are some principles for anyone who deals with children. Not only the parent, but also the coach, teacher, babysitter etc.

What you do matters

This is one of the most important principles. Your kids are watching you. Don't just react on the spur of the moment. Think about your reactions because your kids are bound to do the exact same thing soon.

You can never be too loving

You can never spoil your child with too much love. What we often think of as the product of spoiling a child is never the result of showing a child too much love. It is usually the consequence of giving a child things instead of love — things like leniency, lowered expectations or material possessions.

Be involved in your kid's life

It is hard work to be an involved parent. It often means rethinking and rearranging your priorities. It frequently means sacrificing what you want to do for what your child needs to do. Be there mentally as well as physically. But this does NOT mean doing your child's homework!

Adapt your parenting

Your parenting should fit your child. Keep pace with your child's development. Consider how age is affecting your child's behavior. You can't treat a three-year-old the same as a teenager.

Establish and set rules

You should manage your child's behavior when he is still young, otherwise he will have a hard time learning how to manage himself when he is older and you are not around. The rules your child has learned from you are going to shape the rules he applies to himself. As they grow older, they must be left alone to make their own choices. Parents should not intervene.

Foster your child's independence

Setting limits helps your child develop pa sense of self-control. Encouraging independence helps her develop a sense of self-direction. Both is needed for a successful life. Many parents mistake their child's strive for independence with rebelliousness or disobedience. Children want to become independent because it is part of human nature to want to feel in control rather than to feel controlled by someone else.

Be consistent

Don't let your rules vary from day to day and don't enforce them only intermittently. Your most important disciplinary tool is consistency. Identify your non-negotiables. The more your authority is based on wisdom and not on power, the less your child will challenge it. When parents are not consistent, their children get confused.

Avoid harsh discipline

Parents must never hit a child. They (the children) will end up hitting other children. They will turn out to be bullies and they will think that aggression solves disputes with others. Time-out works better as it does not involve aggression.

Explain your rules and decisions

Every parent has expectations they want their child to live up to. Explain it to your child so that he or she understands it. A young child may need a little more explaining than a teenager. Keep that in mind.

Treat your child with respect

The best way to get respect from your child is when you treat him or her with respect. You should give your child the same courtesies you would give to anyone else. Speak politely; respect their opinions and pay attention when they speak to you. Treat them with kindness and try to please them when you can. Children treat others the way their parents treat them. So your relationship with your child is the foundation for their relationships with others.

Chapter 3: You Survived The Early Years...

Parenting Little Kids, the first part of the parenting series, took us through the first decade of childhood from birth to high school days.Mothers of very young children look forward to the day they can relax their supervision slightly and get some 'me-time'.Bad news is: it never happens!

Okay there are certain advantages when your child has enough years under his belt to be able to get to and from school without you holding his hand, but the actual 'peace and quiet and time' that you were so yearning for when you were racing around changing diapers and going to playgroup – forget it lady, you're locked in for twenty years!You simply exchange one set of priorities for another.

The high school era is glorious, with your kid providing some of the funniest and uplifting moments of your life but it is all still hard work and if you want your kid to reach adulthood with some level of success this is no time to take your foot off the pedal.

By the time children reach high school entry their particular talents have surfaced and if they did not - they probably soon will.Parents with a certain skill set might be delighted to see their own capabilities shining forth in their offspring – and some are bitterly disappointed to find out that their child shows absolutely no aptitude for things in which they themselves excel.

The important thing is to encourage your child in wherever their passionate interests lie – always assuming that the interest is suitable and not likely to inhibit progress.

The Internet Issue

A modern problem that has surfaced in recent decades is that many children show a talent for being able to utilise internet tools to access information their parents might not necessarily feel is appropriate.Apart from the dangers of sexual abuse on the internet there are sites that offer pornography, gambling and online shopping opportunities that you would never permit your child to view if you were given a choice.

One of the main difficulties is that the parent is often less capable than the child in terms of competence on the home PC.Responsible parents will fit a nanny supervision facility with restricted or no access to certain sites but this is rarely enough.No child is going to be able to resist looking at prurient or forbidden material − it is what children do!It is therefore imperative to combine censorship software with physical supervision.Make sure your child uses a computer somewhere you can take an occasional peek over her shoulder – and do not listen to objections.

Music sites and video sites are a particular concern.You might not consider taking your 11-year-old to see an explicit movie but you would be amazed at how much kids can gain access to via their computers.Know that the material is out there and make an effort to not only inform your child that such material is forbidden but also install software to make it as difficult as possible to access.The dangers of allowing children unsupervised access to the internet include not only inappropriate exposure but also the risk of addiction to gambling, pornography and other vices.

Money, Money, Money

From around the age of about six upward you might want your child to begin learning money management.This is a good idea and the younger the better.It begins with a piggy bank and management of weekly pocket money and progresses to having a savings account and also a current account with a cheque book and bank card.

Bear in mind that having a cheque book and a bank card does not automatically imbue a person with the know-how to handle finance.Deposit a little cash to enable your child to move money but putting a large amount of money at the disposal of a young person is not a good idea.They are likely to mishandle it and then face agonies when they are unable to face you and tell you the cash has disappeared!

Internet banking is also a good idea for your child to learn how things are done but again make sure you supervise vigilantly.Be subtle about it and try not to let your kid feel you do not trust him – but supervise all the same.There are thousands of websites offering all manner of booby traps for naïve forays into poor purchasing and investment and some unscrupulous companies actually target youngsters so beware.

Wherever possible it is a good idea to involve kids with the daily shopping for groceries and other household items.One day they will have to share an apartment with others at college or have to strike out on their own – the more practical experience you can provide at this early stage the easier it will be for them when they have to abandon the family nest.

This should cover all aspects of home shopping – and don't forget to show your child how to read supermarket labels and be particular about what they eat – nutrition is no longer a case of throwing salad onto the side of the plate for a nod to healthy eating – you might be surprised to pick up a few pointers yourself along the way!

Chapter 4: Starting an Allowance

It's never too early to start teaching your children about money.A great way to begin this is by giving them an allowance.There are several ways to do this, and I'll talk about a few of them. You can give allowance based on chores with specific money amounts.For example, you can decide to pay fifty cents for setting the dinner table, $1.00 for keeping their bedroom clean all week.

You decide the chores you would like your child to do, and then show them how to do the work correctly.Let them know ahead of time how much they get for each job, and keep track.Decide how often they will receive the money they have earned. Another option is to have a set amount of allowance based on their age.My children earn half their age in allowance.My five year old gets $2.50 a week.In order to earn their allowance, they have to keep their room clean, do an assigned job each day, and help out with other things that we might need.When they don't do jobs or keep their room clean, they lose part of their allowance for the week.

Some parents give their children money without requiring the child to earn it.I don't like this option because I like giving a value to the money.When children have to earn it, it means more to them.However, if you don't like the idea of putting your kids to work, you can still teach them about money.I would still suggest assigning a requirement to the money, such as good grades or good behavior.Whatever option you chose, staring an allowance with your children will teach them about working, how to spend money, and how to save it as well.

Camping with Kids

I remember the days of camping before children.Grab a bag of clothes, sleeping bag and tent, and make a quick stop at the store for some food.My friends and I could plan a camping trip in fifteen minutes and be out the door a half hour later.Camping with kids is a whole different ballgame. Most of the friends I know that camp with their kids have a trailer to sleep in.They have found that this is the easiest route to take.Turning on a generator to run your blow dryer is not my idea of camping.So how can you "rough it" with kids?

This is another great teaching opportunity.Survival.Necessity.Make a list of what you must take to survive your camping trip.Talk to your kids about what is a necessary item.Have them pack these first.Then talk about what they would like to make camping more fun or easier.See if there is room to pack some of these things.Know that food is half the battle.Figure out how you are going to cook your food, and plan accordingly.

You don't want to spend all day cooking, and you don't want to be sitting around the fire at 8:00 at night waiting for that chicken to cook. Don't get caught up in "what are we going to do".You are out in nature!Explore it.Go for walks, find a place to camp by a river or lake, watch the stars, dig in the dirt.Show your children that entertainment can be found in the simple things. Keeping it simple will make your camping trip more fun and less work for you.With a little pre-planning, you can have a great time camping with your kids.

Choosing good Friends

Friends are an important part of childhood and you want to make sure that your child develops good friendships early on.It's easiest to make the best choices for your children while they are young. Have your children invite their friends to play at your house.This gives you a chance to see how they play together and how they interact with other members of your family.Become acquainted with their parents also, and you will find that this will help you understand their family situation.Help your child to understand what your values are and to recognize the same values in friends that they make.

Teach your kids values that are important to you, like being honest, and make sure they understand that it applies to friends too.I had a daughter who came to me because a friend wanted her to lie to me about going to the mall.She told me what she really wanted to do, and what her friend thought she should say.After her friend went home that day, we talked about what makes a good friend.She decided that she didn't want a friend that was going to try to get her to lie. Realize that all children are different.

 You might have a child that has fifteen friends and makes new friends easily.Then you might have another child who only has one or two friends, but has a closer friendship with them.Recognize what works for your child and help them develop the relationships that fit with their own personality. Helping your child understand how to be a good friend will help them recognize good friends also.It is so much easier to influence your children while they are young.Take advantage of these opportunities while you can.

Chapter 5: Being Mature During and After a Divorce

We've all known couples who have gotten divorced and make everyone extremely uncomfortable when they have to come to a family function.The sad part of this is that the children are the ones who really suffer.Every birthday party is spent divvying up time between mom and dad.These parents, who make everyone uncomfortable at family functions, are more focused on themselves than they are on anyone else.They are so embroiled in the conflict and feelings they still have for their ex-spouse that they don't give any thought to the effects they are having on everyone else.The children should not be subjected to this as it will color them for the rest of their lives.Not only will it affect them in their own relationships, but it can also cause resentments towards their parents.

The child may have to have separate birthday parties, separate Christmas celebrations and separate Thanksgiving meals.Some of this is to be expected as each partner goes on with his or her own life.However, the child will continue to feel caught in the middle, especially if one parent is bad mouthing the other.Instead, parents have to learn how to make the separate occasions exciting and stress-free for the child.Children should not feel pulled or guilty about spending a holiday with one parent or the other.Instead, the parents should work this out beforehand so that everyone has access to each other during these special occasions.

Sometimes, there is a level of guilt that hangs over the child when they realize they have to choose who they want to spend important holidays and milestones with.If the parents cannot get along in the same room, this can disrupt all kinds of important moments in the child's life including graduation, birthdays and so forth.

To some extent, this is about maturity.Parents who are unable to have mature conversations and understand that everything isn't about them will likely put a lot of emotional turmoil into the lives of their children.Yes, there are some strong emotions that lead up to a divorce.However, these strong emotions do not give parents the right to drag their children through the mud.At some point, maturity has to take over.Unfortunately, many parents want to get the last word in with their spouse or ex-spouse.They want to argue because they're used to arguing.That has been the customary way of doing things throughout the marriage.

Perhaps there was infidelity or some other major event that caused the divorce.It doesn't really matter.If you're a parent, your child deserves for you to be mature enough not to drag them through the situation.Kids should not be exposed to adult problems.The adults decided to get married, and decided to get divorced.The child should never be penalized for that.

This is why it's so important to understand the mechanics of having a good divorce.Let's talk frankly for a moment.

When you chose your spouse, your child didn't have any say-so over the matter.You may have made a good choice or bad choice, but that still isn't the fault of your child.When you decided to get a divorce from your spouse, that too was not the fault of your child.

Parents have to understand that emotions cannot rule when it comes to co-parenting children after divorce.While you might want to wring the neck of your ex-spouse, you have to develop a level of maturity and restraint out of love for your child.Don't make this about you; make it about the kids.Do everything in your power to be at your best so that your child doesn't have to suffer the consequences of a divorce that wasn't their fault.

Divorce changes the structure of the family from one that lives under the same roof to one that doesn't. However, there are families out there who are navigating the tricky waters by becoming what they refer to as a binuclear family. This means that those parents are doing everything they normally would do including caring for and socializing their children, but they simply don't live in the same home anymore.

It's hard to find healthy models for a good divorce because we see so many dysfunctional situations around us. We're overwhelmed with stories of negativity when it comes to divorce, so it's hard to focus on making your story different.

Above all else, do not talk negatively about your soon to be ex-spouse in the presence of your child. Be very careful that they don't hear you say negative things about their parent. It's not fair, and it's a dirty way to get back at your ex at the expense of your child. Pitting a child against their parent is cruel to both your ex-spouse and the child. Don't be tempted to do this or you will find that your child will resent you for it later.

Another component to this is that you may be the only one in your relationship who is interested in being mature and trying to keep the children emotionally secure. That just means you have to fight even harder because you might be fighting for that alone.

Chapter 6: Why Family Time Matters

As much as you want to financially provide for your kids and give them the materials things that they want, nothing can beat the emotional and verbal support kids need from parents. A lot of kids who have new gadgets, new clothes and basically any material thing they want still feels neglected when their parents aren't there to give them a pat in the shoulder when they do something great or hug them when they feel sad and frustrated.

In fact, researches show that most delinquent teenagers and troublesome kids come from families where they feel neglected, unwanted and unnoticed. They resort to bullying others and cause trouble to feel good. The rush of adrenaline in their bodies and the feeling of authority over someone make them feel noticed and elated. However, the feeling is only momentary. When their parents scold them for their behavior, these kids have the tendency to think that they are only noticed by their parents when they do something wrong. The cycle then goes on and on.

Compare that with children who have involved parents. They tend to do well in school, are more outgoing with good social skills, understanding and appreciative. Even if they aren't well off financially speaking, the love and affection they get from their parents is enough to motivate them to do better. Aside from that, they feel more relaxed, comfortable and happy knowing that they have a warm and happy home to come back to at the end of the day.

There's a big difference in the attitude of children who have involved parents and those who doesn't. Some kids whose parents aren't as involve as others tend to be more distant, cold and misunderstanding towards their parents. They're more likely to become delinquents and troublesome while others get more absorbed and lost in what they do. The reaction is not the same with everyone but the effect is negative. It slowly strips away the kid's enthusiasm and compassion that it also negatively affects others around them.

Family time matters. Be it a few minutes at breakfast or dinner table. It's good for kids when they know that they can talk to their parents about their problems, their dreams and goals in life. Kids want to grow up knowing that there's someone there to hold their hands when they go through rough times and someone who will celebrate with them when they succeed. For kids, the amount of attention you give them may not be enough when you think it is that's why it is important that you have set a common ground with them. This way you can help understand each other better.

CHAPTER 7: STEP DAD STRATEGIES TO BUILD BETTER BLENDED FAMILIES

Step-dads are especially concerned because they are not sure what their new role in the life of step-children should be. Many men are also concerned about how to address the roles of "hers, mine and ours."

Family Meetings Build Cooperation

Parenting is difficult in the most ideal situations (wait a minute...I have never seen an ideal situation, have you) but can be extra stressful when old patterns and new family members merge. The most successful families I have ever met are the ones who have a regular family meeting where everyone has a chance to be heard and participate in decision making.

The tendency of many males is to assume authority and to try to solve problems immediately with their solution. In a democratic family meeting the emphasis is on planning ahead to avoid sticky situations, provide encouragement and solve problems together.

This is in contrast to an emergency meeting or knee jerk decision whenever a crisis appears. In a regular family meeting of all members of a blended family, each member is assured they will have a forum to be heard in a definite time and place each week.

Strategies for Success

Focus on a project so no one feels they are being singled out to speak unless they are comfortable. We gathered at the kitchen table, but put out play dough or paper and markers and allowed everyone to create what ever they felt like during discussions.

Do much more than solve problems or gripe. If someone has a complaint about another family member, it can only be shared if they have tried to work it out together and they then share at least two compliments.

Agree on the distribution of chores and consequences for not having them done at agreed on time.

Express positive feelings and encouragement to family members.

Acknowledge progress of each member.

Plan recreational outings.

Build a team spirit for "our house."

Share feelings and hopes for the future

If some family members decide not to attend family meetings, decisions can still be made by those that are present. We kept a communication log and rotated the role of note keeper. This comes in handy to refer back to decisions, so the step-parent doesn't have to be the bad guy.

You can build a better blended family and I have confidence in you. Children are so hungry for strong role models to teach, mentor and respect them. You are doing an important work as a dad.

Chapter 8: Tips For Building Character

Character is essential for the growth of a child. It comes above everything else as without character, you lose your true self. In order to build character in your child, you must first know your obligation as a parent, which is to provide for, protect, nourish and teach your child. Your joy as a parent is raising up a child who has these six pillars in life which is being respectful, trustworthy, responsible, fair, caring and a good citizen. That is what character is about. Discipline and educating your child has to start early in their life. Without much ado, we are going to look at ways of building character in your child.

Be A Role Model

Bad character corrupts good moral. Unless you as a parent portrays high moral standards, your child can never have good character traits. A child imitates everything that their parents do. In their innocence and unconditional love, whatever you do is what they will take as being the right thing. To begin with, a good method is teaching by example. If you want your child to be respectful, show them respect first, and that is how they will learn. Never use drugs, alcohol or smoke in front of your children because when you tell them that it is wrong, they will never understand and end up doing the same. Avoid having arguments or getting in a fight with your spouse as the child needs to grow knowing that quarreling and getting into fights with other people is not the way to solve conflicts. Lastly, get involved in community work, which will inspire your child and instill tolerance and understanding for other people.

Create Time For Your Child

Spending time with your child is very fulfilling and a step towards building character. Taking time to be with your child will create a bond between the two of you. Your child will not only see you as a parent but also a friend and confidant. This means that they will be honest and trust you to the extent of telling you their secrets. And, as long as you are honest with them, they will be honest with you. They will know that they can trust you with problems that they are dealing with knowing that you will help them get through. When you spend time with your child, they feel loved and this will give them a sense of security. This closeness will enable you to know your child's likes and dislikes. You will get to know what kind of TV programs they watch, music they listen to and the materials they read. This will be helpful in finding out if they are involved in any undesirable activities and you can address the situation or behavior before things get out of hand. When spending time together, take the opportunity to mentor your child to have the values that you cherish.

Make Known Your Values

It is your responsibility to help your child differentiate right from wrong to develop the ability to get along with others. When growing up, your child does not know what is expected of them. Practicing good parenting entails you teaching your son or daughter the virtues and values that are upheld in the society. You can start this by making a list of standards that have to be achieved.

You should therefore sit with your child to discuss your values and how they can incorporate these values in their life. For instance, you can teach them honesty by being truthful and do not make promises that you are not going to fulfill. If you promise to buy them a gift, then buy it and don't come up with excuses. In so doing, your child will also remain honest at all times. If you show your child love, they will show affection and consideration to others in return.

Discipline Your Child Appropriately

Once you clarify the values you want from your child, setting up of rules should follow and failure of your son or daughter to adhere to them should be followed by punishment. How you discipline your child will have a profound effect on how your child grows. The strategies you use to discipline your children will also determine the nature of relationship you will have with the children. The technique you use to discipline your children could also determine the kind of mood they will have and their temperament. For example if your child is on the wrong, don't yell when talking to them, be calm and speak on how you feel when they do something wrong. This will show them that you love them and are looking out for them.

I would also advise that rather than focus on punishing bad behavior, why not put more emphasis on rewarding good behavior. This will reinforce good behavior since your child would not want to do something bad because they would not receive a reward. Over time, the good behaviors become habits ingrained in the child.

Be Consistent

Parenting requires consistency and giving of concrete and clear explanations to your child. As a parent you should learn to use clear language when addressing your child; let your no be no and yes be yes. Your style of parenting should not change depending on your moods and environments. Children need structures and consistency in every way. This however does not mean that you be rigid but rather know when is the best time to be flexible. For instance, even if your child is supposed to sleep at 8pm but wants to spend some time with you, you can compromise and spend a few more minutes with them. It would not do you any good to force them to go to bed when they just miss you since you always come home from work when they are asleep.

Provide Books

Reading is a great way of knowing about other people's experiences, relating them to you and getting ways of coping with situations. At an early age, you should provide reading materials for your child. Apart from being entertaining, storybooks teach on good morals to a large extent. If your child is unable to read because they are too young, you should read to them and interpret but the ultimate goal will be to make sure they have learnt a positive lesson from the story.

Keep Your Child Busy With Suitable Activities

Idleness is what makes children get involved in mischievous behaviors. As a parent, you should observe your child keenly to know what their talents are. Talents need to be nurtured so that they may be productive. After noting your child's talent, take the next step and introduce them to activities in which they will be able to bring out their best. If they have an interest in musical instruments, buy for them a piano, guitar or flute and look for a tutor to help. Having granted your child this, they will be involved both physically and emotionally in a positive activity hence positive character. Going out for nature walks, swimming and playing is involving and thus will keep their minds busy from uncouth behaviors.

Chapter 9: Watch Your Time Fillers

Be honest with yourself. List the things that you use to fill your time. Then list the things that you could be doing with that time, and set some goals for yourself.

Examples are to do a free online short course while you wait for the kids at swimming class, or finish the book you've been wanting to read while they're in the bath, or to answer your emails while you're on the bus so that you can use that time to have a hot candle lit bath in the evenings!

Reward yourself for not wasting your time.

Get Help

Just what help is going to look like is going to be dependent on your situation, on what's available, and on what you need.

It can be as simple as speaking to your minister or priest, or it can be more involved, seeing a counsellor, or longer-term mental health care.

There is no shame in needing help.

In fact, being brave enough to stand up and say that you need help is a huge positive step in coming out the other end of 'tough times'.

When my mother died, I had a free weekly counselling session at the local cancer charity. They couldn't solve my problem. They didn't take away my pain. It wasn't until months after I'd left that I realised that I was suffering from some post-traumatic stress, but it had provided a space where I could **talk.** No one was going to judge me, and no one was going to tell me what to do. I could just **talk.**

Whether it's post-marriage counselling, a coffee with a friend who has been there, a child-minder for two hours a week so you can have a long hot bath, or a professional relationship, getting help isn't weakness.

Create an emotional first aid kit for yourself: the names and numbers of people you could call on when you need them – people you might not choose in the moment of pain, but know in your heart you **could** call. Keep some Rescue Remedy and a copy of your affirmations in it. Your notes from this book will help too.

Activity 13: Get Help

Make a list of the resources you could call on when you need it. List the people who can help you with child care. Add their numbers if need be. Add your counsellor's number, and add your membership number, booking number, patient number – whatever you might need, so that you don't have to be searching for it when you're struggling. List friends who you know in your heart you could call when you need someone but know you might not think of when you feel like you're falling apart.

Remember Who You Are

You are first and foremost, you. You are a person, a human. You are flawed, you are fallible, you are normal.

Whatever you're facing, you are allowed to have feelings about.

No, you're not the first person to lose a loved one. You're not the first to be cheated on. You're not the first to end up on benefits by no fault of your own.

And you won't be the last.

But that doesn't mean that you aren't allowed to have feelings about it.

You're allowed to be angry – but not to hurt others in your anger. You're allowed to be sad – but not to destroy yourself or others in your sadness.

You're allowed to feel whatever you want, because this is **your** story. This is **your** journey. This is **your** life.

But you don't have to let it swallow you. And as a parent, you can't let it. Because there is someone always watching. Watching how you deal with your suffering, and how you deal with your pain.

They cannot understand it. They cannot feel it in the way that you do. But it's in the hardest parts of our lives that we equip our children for dealing with the hardest parts of their own.

If you've 'failed' in your parenting ideals, remember that your children don't know that. To them, whatever you present to them is normal. They don't know the expectations we hold as we whisper promises to our new born babies. They only know what we give them.

And they only know what we show them. So if you've had a bad day, if you've yelled and said mean things and thrown their toys in the bin, and been wholly unreasonable because of **your own suffering**, it's okay to say sorry. It's okay to ask them for a hug and to tell them that you are struggling and that you could do with a little extra love.

For most children, especially smaller ones, the invitation to show love will always be accepted. Showing them when we're vulnerable will generally be met with gentleness, and understanding.

I remember one particular day. I had **no** money in the bank. I had no access to money. And our cupboards were decidedly bare. Our local home education/schooling group was having an Easter Egg Hunt, and everyone was to bring eggs to join in the hunt.

In tears I told my children we could go to the session, but we wouldn't be able to collect eggs as I didn't have the £2 for eggs, or we could stay home and do something together. My six year old daughter looked up at me with her big, beautiful eyes and said "Mama, we don't need eggs. We can go and play with our friends, but don't worry, we don't need eggs." Her compassion and understanding blew me away.

As it happened there was a surplus of eggs and they got to have some anyway, which made my day but the blessing of her kindness stuck with me.

Our children know who we are, probably better than anyone else. There's no harm in showing them when we are having a hard time, and allowing them to be a part of our healing.

Chapter 10: AGES AND STAGES

The most critical part of a child's life – the first five years – is under the control of you, the parents. By 'control' I mean that you have the opportunity – and the obligation – to profoundly shape your child's development. Children don't simply grow up by themselves – and when they do, it's almost guaranteed that bad things will happen. What you do with your children determines how they will respond to other people, how well they do in school, and what successes they will have – or not – in their lives. This is a tall order, but it boils down to a few basic – but critical – principles which we'll talk about. And I'll give you some places to find information and help along the way.

As parents we are in charge of the growth stages our children go through; and in charge of their activities, known as "developmental play." This sounds pretty silly....of course parents take care of their kids while they grow and play! But most of us didn't know how important it is to grow and play during those first five years. The Center on the Developing Child at Harvard University calls it developing the "architecture of the brain."

In their ground-breaking research, they tell us that 700 new neural connections are made every second during the first few years of life – 700 every second! – faster than at any other time in our lives. These connections are made through a child's relationships with parents and significant others, and their experiences (good and bad) within their environment.

While it seems that "…all they do is play…" during their first five years, playing is actually a child's work; and is crucial for physical health, intellectual stimulation, social/emotional development, and interpersonal skills. Play is how children learn language, develop their executive functions for logic and planning, learn how to take risks and deal with failure, and increase their self-confidence and positive self-esteem.

Each child develops at their own rate, and will demonstrate greater skill in some areas than in others as they go through the various socialization stages of play; but the developmental sequence is the same. Play forms the basis for success in language and academics, and developing coping skills and resilience by falling down and getting up again in a secure environment.

The first five years of life are important because the early experiences that kids have, positive and negative, make a huge impression on their 'new' brains and bodies. Look at it this way – we know that an infant's skin is far more sensitive to the sun than an adults because it hasn't been exposed enough to the sun; but over time it becomes tougher.

Much the same is true of the rest of a child's body, their brain, and their emotions – while none of us is born as a blank slate, our 'new' brains develop new pathways very fast, and these pathways are very sensitive to new information.

This does not mean that you have to be the perfect parent, but it does mean you need to pay attention to your children's needs from infancy onward. By the time they reach school age, the trajectory of their future growth is set; and problems are much harder to fix.

Everyone has experienced the Terrible Twos, the Inquisitive Threes and the hormonal teenage years; but as young parents, very few understand that cognitive, social and emotional capabilities are inextricably linked throughout our lives with our genetic makeup and physical development. Influences begin prenatally, and provide a good, or not so good, foundation for future development.

The foundations for healthy development are positive love and affection for social and emotional growth; good nutrition for healthy bodies, as well as for healthy brain development; and positive, safe environments where a child's needs are met – i.e., you love your children enough to give them the right foods and a safe, positive home.

Chapter 11: Marriage – Kids – Divorce

Divorce is really about letting go, breaking ties and moving on. This causes a lot of stress and anxiety (especially when kids are involved). It is about journeying into the unknown, uncertain and un-chartered waters and territory. In America, statically 50% percent of first marriages, 67% of second and 74% of third marriages end in divorce.As I reflect back over a five year period I attended approximately 30 weddings of friends, co-workers, family and acquaintances. Out of those wedding only (2) couples are still married and all of them at least one child.On average, first marriages end in divorce within about eight years.I interviewed several of the divorced couples in an effort to analyze the root cause of why their marriage failed. Many of the responses were different yet had similarities and were based on communication, unrealistic expectations, money, unfaithfulness and sex. Some of the responses in those categories were:

Communication:

Lack of communication between spouses; one or both parties took the silent routine when attempting to discuss problem(s)

Will not discuss feelings, personal issues

Keep resentments simmering

Unable to manage or resolve conflict

Personality differences

Criticism

Commitment:

One of the partners in the marriage was not committed enough to work wholeheartedly

One spouse was willing to make sacrifices, while the other one was not

Finance:

Financial decisions were often made without the one of the spouse's knowledge

Both spouses were not equally involved in money matters regardless of who make the most money

Unequal financial status

Undisclosed financial status

Unwilling to stick to a budget

Sex:

The hot and steamy sex disappeared from relationship

Sexual incompatibility

Sexual abuse

Quality of closeness, intimacy, and sex

Sexual disinterest

Unfaithfulness:

One of the spouses unfaithful in the marriage

Unwilling to seek counseling for being unfaithful

Unrealistic Expectations:

Expectations of one of the other spouse were more then they were capable of living up to

Tension, stress, harsh words, conflict, fights, arguments, emotions ran rampant and patience began to wear thin over the smallest things

Incompatibility

As time passed the couples tended to drift farther and farther apart and eventually ended up in divorce court. Divorce leads to a new and different set of problems. So really what changed in the relationship after marriage? The answer is life; after marriage many of the couples had children, careers and the many responsibilities that go along with it and suddenly found themselves caught up in the day to day problems and fail to communicate effectively, be attentive and focus on each other.

After a divorce the ex-spouses should be working together with the kids to embark, reclaim and build a new separate life. This must be done while providing stability and emotionally support for the kids, despite feeling as if your world crumpling before your eyes. Both of the ex-spouses must embrace the future with a positive attitude, hope and a plan of action. Divorce and parenting can be tough, but it's manageable if both ex-spouses keep an open mind as well as effective communication.

Discussing Divorce With Your Children

Children need to understand that they bear no responsibility for their parents getting a divorce. Both parents should emphasize how much they love the children and will continue to be an important part of their lives; therefore, both spouses should sit down with the children to discuss the issue of divorce. This should never be done by only one of the parents because a united front needs to be displayed from the start of the divorce. All of the details of why the divorce is occurring do not need to be shared with the children. Parents should however, make an effort to share as much basic information as possible, although no definite arrangements have been made. Do not allow the discussions to turn into a blame game, simply tell them that the divorce is occurring and explain how it is going to affect them.

The children will most likely be overwhelmed by the news so give them time to adjust. It's a good idea to schedule another meeting in a couple to weeks to discuss how your children are feeling about the divorce. Some children are going to act out in anger over the divorce so be prepared to deal with those emotions. Parents should come to terms with the divorce before approaching the children because too many parents are too wrapped up in their own feeling to provide the moral support that their children need.

The involvement of the children tends to make the transition better for them and they don't fell thrown away in the process. Divorce is never easy but it especially hard when children are involved; however it can be manageable if both spouses are willing to put aside their differences for the betterment of the children.

Chapter 12: Starting Every Day with a Healthy Breakfast in a Fast-Paced World

Start every morning with a hearty, healthy breakfast that will power your children through the rest of the day.Breakfast is, after all, the most important meal of the day, so be sure to provide your children with options that include whole grains for sustained energy, fruits and juices for antioxidants, low-fat milks for calcium, and eggs or even tofu for protein.

Enjoy breakfast together as a family, and try to eat wholesome, natural, organic foods that are free of harmful pesticides that are detrimental to young bodies.If you eat breakfast together, not only do you bond as a family, you also reinforce the importance of starting each day in a healthy way, with foods that energize and provide strength, rather than foods that are loaded with preservatives and unhealthy sugars. Whether your children are getting ready to head off to school or they are on their summer vacation, it is vitally important to always have a great breakfast that will provide the nutrients which will wake them up and give them the energy they need to handle the challenges of schoolwork or a fun day at the beach or pool.And breakfast is especially important for keeping students alert during the school hours before lunch, when they will need to be prepared for classroom discussions, activities, and tests.If a child does not get a good breakfast to start off the day, he/she will feel sluggish, unable to concentrate, and unwilling to perform any physical activities.

Setting Up Play Dates for Your Children to Encourage True Social Growth

Play dates are a perfect way to get your very young children active both socially and physically.And the bonus to play dates is that they are set up with parents in mind, because you can set up play dates around your schedule, with your friends who have children, or with the parents of children with whom your child goes to school.Even children as young as toddlers can benefit from play dates, where they get to mingle with other children who are the same age, playing games together and learning how to share and communicate properly.

Play dates are also a great opportunity for children to learn how to be away from their parents comfortably before they enter pre-school or elementary school.Because many children become attached to their parents when they are very young, they can experience severe separation anxiety and stress when they are sent off to school to be without their parents.But play dates are a fun way to get your child used to being around others, even people who are brand new in his/her life.Your child will learn how to deal with these new experiences in a productive and positive manner, by making friends, establishing relationships with individuals who are not family, and learning important skills that will be valuable both in the classroom and outside of it. From physical activity to mental stimulation, children do extremely well when their parents are involved in setting up play dates from a very young age.

Chapter 13: The Meaning of Tantrum Toddler

Tantrum is a fit of temper or simply put an outburst of anger, mostly a child-like display of bad temper or rage (Encarta dictionary 2007).Also, it is an emotional outburst mostly associated with toddlers or people in emotional distress. Toddler tantrum usually comes in different forms. But they are commonly characterized by crying, stubbornness, anger ranting, defiance, screaming, even up to resistance to pacification attempts and also hitting in some cases. Toddlers in the middle of a tantrum normally lose their physical control and find it difficult to remain calm. This unusual fit of anger is highly common in children from 1 to 3 years. Experiencing this situation for the first time as a parent can put you off and make you react wrongly. That is why most first time parents usually find it difficult to hold on to avoid having a meltdown in the process.

Toddler temper tantrum is an emotional state synonymous to a summer storm. That is coming by sudden and even becoming violent in some cases. In a short while, you are in a restaurant with your child eating dinner and making merry, before you know it she has started, whining, whimpering or even screaming on top of her voice simply because of something as minor as her straw getting bent. As a first time parent, you should start expecting this kind of experience when your child turns 18 to 36 months. You may feel as if you are raising a stubborn child or tyrant when your children begin to display this kind of attitude. Just know that at an early age your child is only having a meltdown as means of response to difficulty and frustration.

 Furthermore, despite the fact that tantrums are in most cases regarded as an enemy of children social behavior, it is good you know that in most case tantrum is just appropriate sign that your child is experiencing frustration excessively owing to her age. When all things are equal, the situation will certainly minimize with calm as well as consistent handling. Parents are the ones to try as much as they can to contain their child when she cannot contain herself due to tantrum. In some case what the child needs that is causing frustration to her may be what she truly requires.

According to a Dallas-based clinical psychologist and a co-author of Simple Strategies That Turn off the Tantrums, Create Cooperation and Try and Make Me! Ray Levy Ph.D. "Meltdowns are terrible, nasty things, but they're a fact of childhood.Levy also explained that toddlers between the ages of 1 to 4 tend to lose their coping skill instead of learning them. Also, he says that a tantrum usually set in as a result of children not getting what they really want or require. For that reason, when your child between the ages of 1 to 4 begins to show bad temper or find it difficult to cope with a difficult situation or lack, you should know that there is something he needs which he either does not have enough or have at all.

What First Time Parents Need To Know About Tantrum Toddler

Are you a first-time parent and wonder why your child usually loses her temper suddenly? Do you find it difficult holding yourself not to have a meltdown when your child is in the middle of a tantrum? Or you are scared of raising a tyrant in your home due to the childish display of bad temper or rage by your child? In case these are your plight, you can end your worries, as you will get solutions here. What you should know is that your child is still normal but passing through a proper stage in the life of every human being. Children between the ages of 18 to 36 months are prone to tantrum, and there is nothing anyone can do about it. You as a parent will not be able to stop it rather what you have to do is to find out how to avoid situations that usually result to tantrum. Though tantrum or child's hissy fit can be discouraging and even embarrassing, you should know that it is absolutely normal for every child. No need to worry about the social behavior of your child at this age unless the problem persists after the child has already gone beyond age 4.

There are certain things first time and frustrated parents do not know about tantrum, and that is why they usually get confused in the process. The things parents need to know about tantrum toddler is categorized into six groups in this book, and they are:

1. Hissy fit is normal but should not be a daily affair: While hissy fit or tantrum is normal for toddlers, it is not an everyday issue. So, you should not be concerned when your child only gets in a tantrum occasionally. Nevertheless, if the fit of temper happens daily or becomes more frequent and predictable like when she does not want to get dressed or is really tired then, you should consult your doctor. Your doctor will be able to rule out certain possible psychology conditions that can be responsible for that.

2. Tantrums Normally go in the expected pattern: Tantrums may resemble pure chaos, but they are more like a symphony, with expected peak and trough. They are also in phases with phase one involving screaming and yelling, phase two involving throwing either oneself on the floor or object. The escalation of phase two is always a sign that phase three is about to begin and phase three usually involve whining and crying. While waiting till phase three before consoling and comforting the tantrum toddler is necessary, the problem is how to bear the aggravation in the phase one and two.

3. Trying to reason with tantrum toddler is a waste of time: If you have a child in the middle of a tantrum, you will discover that begging or reasoning with the child can fuel up the entire situation. The reason is that children in the middle of a tantrum are usually taxed and trying to appeal to their sense of logic will only make matters worse. That is why you should not bother telling your child why she should get dressed before going outside. Instead, you should make short orders such as "be quiet" "sit down" or simply "head to your room."

4. Just ignore the tantrum, and it will cease with time: If you want to end outburst, the best thing is to ignore the scene. Just try as much as you can to turn your back towards your child and do as if you do not notice his whining, crying or screaming and the situation will calm faster. Keeping quiet is a way of refusing to fuel the outburst though it is more difficult to do than just saying it. If you can try to maintain quietness without getting disturbed emotionally or angry, the tantrum will cease within few minutes.

5. Toddler tantrum can surface in various types: Another thing first-time parents need to know about tantrum or hissy fit is that it does surface in toddlers in several types. They are basically grouped into three kinds. There is "**Attention Tantrum**" which is when your child that was formally playing quietly starts yelling or disturbing immediately you decide to talk to someone on the phone. The second type is known as "**Tangible Tantrum,** " and it usually erupts when your child desire or long for something she cannot have such as chocolate or candy bar at a nearby store. The third type is called "**Command avoidance tantrum**" and it typically in the form of stubbornness. This type occurs when your child refuses to change or stop what he is doing even at your command. The command can be as simple as going to bed or taking a bath. While you can handle the first two tantrums by keeping quiet owing to the fact that the child just needs your attention, the third type requires forceful tone and action. Just give the child time to do your command and ensure you put your hand to help them do it when they do not meet up with the time. Since toddlers do not like such help, they will try to avoid it next time.

6. It's OK to admit defeat in some conditions: While handling tantrum toddler, it is important not to be rigid as that can make the child feel bad and unloved. Like when you are in between two opinions like preparing to go somewhere only for your child to start requesting for candy on a stick. In that situation, the best solution is simply to dance to her tune so as to end the sanity. Make sure you do not deny the child her request and admit defeat later. This will easily teach your child that she will have what she want if you are adequately persistent.

The Negative Effects of Tantrum in Toddlers

Several research and studies have been made by many scholars on Tantrum toddlers. Some have tried to find out whether or not there is a negative effect associated with toddler tantrum. Most of the researches made it clear that toddler tantrum is just a normal way of a child showing frustration over a particular situation. Toddler tantrum comes in a certain stage in the life of every child, which makes them a normal experience. However, there are certain negative effects that can manifest itself in several ways in the life of toddlers. You will find out about them through this book. There are things you need to be aware of while managing a toddler that is in the middle of a tantrum. There is a need for every parent mostly the first time parents to keep a close watch on their children to observe all their moves and behaviors while they are in the midst of a hissy fit. There are some signs that indicate that your toddler's tantrum has gone beyond normal occurrences and showing some underlying psychiatric disorders according to recent researches. According to Andy C. Belden and his colleague Washington University researchers, while toddler tantrums are always unbearable to parents, there are about five hissy fit styles that are regarded as "red flags" indicating toddlers mental health issues. It is true that tantrum is normal for toddlers, but it is also important for the parents to watch over their toddler and find out what she is doing at any point in time. Below are five observed "Red Flags" to toddler tantrum which every parent need to take note of:

☐ **Self-Injury**: There is no doubt about the fact that toddlers in the middle of tantrum may hurt themselves in a way to show their aggression over a frustration. But when that becomes a norm or continues to take place up to 90 to 95%, it may be an indication of major depression, disruptive behavior or even mixed major depression.

Most toddlers with this mental health issues always scratch themselves, bite themselves, kick objects nearby and even bang their head on the wall in a way to injure themselves. The issue with toddler tantrum is that most first time parents usually misunderstand or even ignore some signs that are clear indicative that their toddler has a mental issue. So, as a parent, it is important for you to keep an eye close to your toddler that is in the middle of a tantrum so as to know when the situation is going out of the ordinary.

☐ V**iolence towards objects, minder or even both**: Paying close attention to the behavior of your child while in the middle of a tantrum is of great importance. It is true that tantrum toddlers usually get hostile or violent and can transfer that to anyone around them, but there is a limit to it. In fact, if your toddler shows violence towards the minder or objects and it happened concurrently for some weeks or even months, it can be a sign of a destructive disorder. There is no doubt of the fact that tantrum toddlers sometimes kick against their mother simply because she refused to buy them cookies, but if this happens up to 90%and to the extent you would be hiding yourself to avoid being injured, then you have to take your toddler to a doctor for checkup.

☐**Very Long Tantrum:** No parent loves a tantrum especially when it is in public. For that reason, a tantrum lasting up to five minutes can seem like so many years to first-time parents. However, toddlers that have tantrum more than 25 minutes consistently should be checked as that can be a sign of mental disorder. It is true that a normal toddler's tantrum can last longer up to an hour but not like that always. Rather a normal toddler tantrum can take an hour today but only take 30 seconds the next time.

☐**Frequent Tantrum:** If your toddler starts having 10 to 20 tantrums at home within one month or above 5 tantrums daily on several days outside the home, it could be a sign of a psychiatric problem which should be handled with immediate effect. You should not allow the problem to linger to avoid it regenerating to something more serious that may end up affecting the social behavior of your child in the future.

☐**Lack of the Ability to Calm Ones-Self after Tantrum:** Normal toddler tantrums do not always require an external force to make the child calm. Sometimes you as a parent may have to bribe the toddler in order for her to calm down but that should not be all the time. As the matter of facts, if your toddler lacks the will power or ability to calm down after many hours of a tantrum, you should take him to a psychiatrist for a mental checkup.

Chapter 14: How to Mentally Prepare To Deal with Your Growing Toddler

Having children can be one of the greatest joys in the world. Children add a great deal to our lives especially when a new baby arrives. However, a baby quickly grows and they will soon develop into a toddler. It is important for a parent to mentally prepare themselves to deal with their growing toddler.

A baby is so precious and so very tiny. A baby heavily relies on their mother to feed them, bathe them, change their diapers and put them safely to bed. Once a baby becomes a toddler it can be much more challenging for a parent in a variety of ways.

A baby can be referred to a toddler when they are between the ages of 1-2. Normally, when a baby begins to walk they are considered to be a toddler. A parent will more than likely experience a period of adjustment when their child is a toddler.

Dealing with a toddler can be difficult in some ways. Toddlers can be more difficult especially due to the fact that they are now able to walk. In addition, between ages 1-2 toddlers begin to articulate certain words and phrases.

When a toddler begins to walk, this changes the whole scheme of things for a parent. The parent has to watch the child more closely than ever before. A toddler is normally curious and may tend to explore different areas of the home.

Keep in mind toddlers have no sense and they need guidance from a parent or authority figure each and every day of their lives.

A toddler may investigate by opening dresser drawers looking for whatever they can find. Therefore, it is important for a parent to place anything that could be considered dangerous out of reach. For example, if needles or hair pins were normally stored in a certain table or drawer it may be time to move these items to higher ground.

A parent can mentally prepare for a situation like this by moving dangerous items including breakables to a locked cabinet. It is best to convince yourself that until your toddler gets through this particular stage of life that your general everyday life will definitely change at least for a while.

The majority of toddlers experience what many call "the terrible two's". By age two toddlers are essentially into everything. Toddlers will open drawers, grab anything that they can get their hands on and they may break a number of glass objects. For a two year old breaking glass items and going through drawers is a form of entertainment. In addition, a two year old child is naturally curious about their surroundings.

Even though toddlers' actions may be termed as "normal" it can still be quite difficult for the parents and other family members. Essentially, toddlers between the ages of 1-2 are developing a mind of their own and their true personality may begin to shine through.

In addition to curiosity, a toddler may also start to develop irregular sleeping habits. The days may be long gone when a parent puts their baby to bed for a good night's rest. A toddler may no longer go right to sleep when they are put to bed. Therefore, a parent may have to change their agenda when dealing with their toddler.

Sleeping habits are not the only thing that may be changing. Toddlers begin to develop different tastes. Babies are normally easy to feed due to the fact they will eat just about anything when hungry. A toddler may develop fussy eating habits which can also produce some stress on the parent.

Parents may have to experiment with different foods to find something that their toddler will enjoy eating. This is normally not a big deal however; all in all it is a big change for both toddler and parent. A parent can best prepare for this particular situation by buying different foods in an attempt to find something their toddler will enjoy eating.

Keeping a toddler entertained can become more difficult. Therefore, it may be helpful if the toddler has a variety of toys and stuffed animals close by. In addition, toddlers are normally quite responsive to pleasant music. Pleasant music can help to keep a toddler entertained and it may also help them to go to sleep.

Toddlers have the tendency to wander away from their parents if the opportunity presents itself. Therefore, it is critical that the parent keep a close watch on their toddler at all times. If a toddler runs away from a parent then the parent has to teach the toddler what the word "no" means.

Just as parents must prepare themselves for the arrival of a new baby, parents must also mentally prepare themselves for the daily adventures in the life of a toddler.

A parent may benefit greatly by reading books that pertain to toddlers. Books of this nature can help parents to make necessary adjustments to their daily lives. In addition, the books can help a parent better understand what to expect from their toddler especially during the difficult periods.

In addition to books, it may help parents to seek advice from a physician as well as family and friends. A pediatrician can guide a parent on how to better cope with their toddler.

Toddlers can be unpredictable. The behavior of a toddler can change dramatically from one day to the next. A parent must learn to adapt to the changing behavioral patterns of their toddler.

Dealing with a growing toddler can take a great deal of mental preparation. Caring for a toddler on a daily basis can be enjoyable but at the same time physically and mentally draining.

By making some changes and modifications to your daily routine you should be able to deal with the changing behavior and growing needs of your toddler.

No one ever said that raising a child would be easy. A toddler can demand a great deal of time and attention from a parent particularly the mother. However, once a child gets through the toddler years their life should become more settled and hopefully more manageable for the parents.

Chapter 15: Tone and Body Language

Why Our Tone and Body Language Speak Louder Than Our Words Alone

"Actions speak louder than words"

Indeed. Our words do matter but that doesn't make our actions any less important. One thing necessary in conveying the right message to your receiver is "cohesiveness." This would refer to how compact and consistent the message you're trying to get across is.

Imagine someone saying sweet words to you with furrowed brows. Or, your husband telling you he's not mad whilst clenching his fists or locking his arms across his chest. In these situations, you instantly doubt if they mean what they say. Children too, no matter how young, can spot these incongruences and sense the insincerity behind those words.

When you're telling your kids that they're doing a great job, allow your gestures to show them exactly how you feel as well. When you feel angry, try to talk after you've calmed down. It can make children feel uneasy hearing your calming words accompanied by tension in your voice. We may be well-intentioned, but kids can sense something is not right. This way of communicating will most likely send them mixed signals and they'd be troubled over how they should be interpreting it.

What's In A Tone?

Words alone have less of an impact if not accompanied by the appropriate tone. No matter how grandiose a speech is, it'll never leave anyone a deep impression if delivered in monotone; a single, heartfelt sentence conveyed with a sincere tone will always be more impactful.

A tone therefore, is the soul of your words. It gives depth and impression to what you say. That is why when speaking to children, let us be extra careful with the tone of our voice. Let's make a greater effort to match the words we say with the appropriate tone so that we can connect with our children on a whole different level.

I have this friend (I won't name names) who is well-intentioned, but likes to use sarcasm, even with her young kids. Sarcastic remarks such as "You did a really fine job ruining my mood by throwing your toys all over the place" were used. She assumed her kids would understand that she is trying to be nice and at the same time, learn to keep their toys in the drawers after use. However, that has little effect besides confusing the hell out of her kids.

I've learnt from hearing her experience, and I realized if we have something important to say, make sure to word it in a direct and sincere manner.

On the other hand, there are also instances when we mean good but our children take it the wrong way. You could be saying "I'm so proud of you", but in a very dry manner that it hardly makes your kid feel motivated! From the examples above, we can sense the importance of our tone in either making or breaking a conversation.

The Impact Of Body Language

Every part of our body has something to say. When we're happy, our lips curved into a smile. When we're sad, our eyes tear up. When we're angry, our feet stomp.

By observing one's body language, we can come up with a pretty accurate guess as to the emotional state the person is in. It is often said that in communication, body language accounts for 55% of the overall message (4)!

For us to communicate effectively with our children, let's avoid the following movements:

Pointing fingers — When our little ones misbehave, it is our duty as a parent to instill proper discipline in them. However, we sometimes have this tendency to point our index finger at them when trying to emphasize our point. For example, when we say "I can't believe you broke my phone" while pointing at them. The child can interpret that gesture as something we use to identify the person at fault in a situation. It may give them the idea to blame others for their own faults by pointing their fingers at them thereby absolving themselves of any wrongdoing.

Turning your back while they're trying to communicate something – When a child has something to say, it is ideal to keep yourself in an open position. This is achieved by facing the child, with your eyes leveled (if possible), and your arms and legs relaxed. A big no is to turn to the other direction while your child is still trying to express something. Next thing you know, they'll be doing this to you too!

Shushing – Generally speaking, shushing – putting your index finger on top of your closed lips – doesn't do children any harm.

It's simply an indication that they have to quiet down or behave themselves while something important is going on. However, similar to the "turning your back" gesture, it's best to avoid using it when the child is still telling you about something that's important to him or her, unless there's really an emergency and you have to cut the conversation for a while. This is because we'll want to give our children ample space and patience as they form the right words to express their feelings.

Making faces – Even though we're now parents ourselves, there are still times when our childish selves resurface. Most parents probably would have made funny faces to make our babies giggle. But some of us just can't get enough of our kids' adorableness that we keep doing it up until they're 2 or 3 years old. Urging them to cry with a sad face or making them angry with a mocking face gets us all giddy especially with their cute reactions.

Beware! This seemingly-innocent teasing can backfire against you. You might be surprised when you get a mocking face during one of your 'sermons'. Kids sure know how to give epic payback!

Instead of making faces, let's try the following instead:

Smiling – And not just any smile. Always give them a genuine smile that comes from deep within your heart. When they do something that's pleasing, make sure to let them know. Give them affirmation by saying "Awesome job!" with a happy tone in your voice and a bright smile on your face.

Give them lots of hugs– My boys always love it when they get huge hugs from their Dada – more than getting ones from me, actually! Children feel secure when they get hugs and embraces from people they trust the most. Make it a point to free your Sunday evenings and just go have some snuggling time with the whole family while watching your favorite shows on TV. That simple act goes a long, long way!

Thumbs-up! -Nothing says "good job" more than a big thumbs-up! Kids like to get approval from their parents, especially when they do something noteworthy. Be sure to give them the okay not only through words but through gestures as well.

A gentle pat on the head – This is a warm gesture to show children whenever they realize their mistakes and feel guilty about them. This gesture is also very comforting for your little ones who feel down or disappointed for some reason. It's a way of showing that you're always going to be there for them no matter what. Again, this makes your kids feel safe, and it can only bring you closer to one another!

A rub on the back – When your child is feeling shy or has little confidence in what he or she is about to do, a little rub on the back or a slight push should give them a quick power boost. It's as if you're saying "Just go have fun. I've got your back!"

I hope that this chapter has illustrated the importance of cohesiveness in our communication with our kids.

Chapter 16: Our Ever Changing Role In How To Be A Good Parent

Seems like it was only a short time ago our kids were learning how to eat, crawl and walk. Now they have their own friends, are going to school and we run the wheels off the mini van taking them to all of the activities that they participate in on a regular basis. As they spread their wings and become independent our ever changing role of being a good parent is to learn how to let go. By developing new strategies you can watch them grow and mature from what they have learned.

They now have their own personality and temperament that is uniquely theirs. Unconsciously your parenting skills were reshaped to accommodate the needs of your children. It has been said that no two children are alike and you realize this more than ever now as you watch them continue to grow. Some kids need more guidance and are not quite as sure of themselves as their brother, sister or their friends. We still must consistently encourage, lead and guide them down the right paths that re-enforces their new found independence. Don't forget to give praise where praise is due which also helps in building their self esteem. But beware, another child may be self-motivated, not need a great deal of help and has the ability to ask for help when needed.

Two of the most important built in tools we can use to modify our parenting skills are our eyes and ears. The ability to truly hear what our children are telling us and seeing what they are doing is invaluable for us to know what they really want or need. For them to be independent it's important to give them feedback and encouragement while still being there for them if or when they might need us. They may not need us to be totally involved with their academic aspirations for success. Instead they may need some social support as they may not be as secure or are scared meeting new people or making friends.

Our ever changing role in how to be a good parent requires that as our kids grow up and change so must our parenting skills change. We must utilize two-way communication; expand their self esteem; make them feel important with encouragement and praise; use positive discipline to instill good behavior; be a good listener; ensure they make good choices; let them play; have a hobby; give them regular hugs and spend quality time to completely connect with your children.

Chapter 17: Helping Your Child Realize His Or Her Talents

Tons of People in the world are clueless about their strengths or talents. This is because often times, parents, or guardians never take time to help children realize what they were good at, or what attracted them.

When your child is unaware of his talents, he or she is likely to follow the path you set out for him or her, or something popular. Soon, your child feels lost and ends up blaming you for not helping him or her explore him or herself. If you do not want your child to reach a point where he or she blames you for failing to help him or her recognize his or her talent, you must then help your child figure out what he or she is good at, and what excites him or her.

How To Help Your Child Recognize His Or Her Talents

Let us look at the different things you need to do to help your child realize his or her hidden talents and potentials.

Do not Impose Your Choice: Before employing effective strategies to discover your child's gifts, you need to bear one thing clearly in your mind. Whatever you do, you must not impose your choice on your child.

Most parents make decisions for their children instead of allowing children the freedom to control their life; these parents have decided what career paths their children should take, what college they should attend, and other important decisions. If you do the same with your child, you are not doing your child any good.

At first, since your child sees you as the authority figure, he or she is less likely to look up to you. However, your child is likely to feel suffocated by your dominating behavior if you don't let them choose and will thus blame you for feeling throttled.

You love your child, and always do what is in his or her interest. However, allow your child a chance to control his or her life. Deciding everything for your child takes that right away and paves the path towards your child's failure. Remember that "As a parent, you have a choice: you will either be the reason your child fails or succeeds, YOU CHOOSE."

Make the right choice for your child by never imposing your decisions. When you avoid imposing ideas on your child, the child gets a chance to explore his or he own inner self, and find out what he or she is truly best at.

Expose your child to various activities at a young age: Expose your child to a variety of interesting activities and subjects at a tender young age so you can give your child many options and activities to become involved in. This will in turn help your child find out what he or she is good at.

For instance, let your child participate in artistic activities, music, sports, literature and culinary activities. Give your child different books to read, and take him or her out to see puppet shows and other activities of this sort.

Doing this opens your child's mind to different possibilities and activities. It helps your child discover interesting things to do and take interest in various activities. You must observe your child's interest and behavior closely to find out what draws his or her interest

In addition, you should make a point of noticing what your child is good at, so that you can encourage him or her to better this skill, passion, or other activities that excite him or her.

Take an interest in your child's blabber: Your child's incessant talk might seem like nonsense right now, but it actually could be something valuable. Listen to everything your child tells you because it could give you clues regarding your child's likes, dislikes, and interests.

If your child incessantly talks about a topic and there is a sparkle in the child's eye, dig deeper into that idea because it could help you discover your child's true gift. You need to be attentive to what your child says even when it doesn't interest you because as a parent, it is your duty to nourish your child's ideas and make your child feel special, which is possible only when you listen to your child's interests and take interest in it.

Find the sparks: Sparks are skills and interests you enjoy. Look for the sparks that make your child happy. Research has validated that sparks birth from your gut. They can be athletic, academic, intellectual, relational, and musical.

A spark can be anything from beautifully playing the piano, to being good at working with senior citizens. Recognizing your child's sparks sets the direction for your child, and helps them achieve their goals and desires easily.

Moreover, the moment your child realizes his or her spark, he or she figures out the 'purpose' of his or her life. Hence, your goal is to identify the sparks in your child, and fuel this spark and infinitely multiply it.

Appreciate your child: Once you recognize a spark in your child, whether this spark is a subject that excites your child, or an innate ability in your baby, you need to appreciate them.

Tell your child how proud you are of him or her, and how amazing he or she is. Appreciating your child with kind words encourages your child to continue dreaming and creating goals related to his or her special gifts and talents.

Polish your child's abilities: Curate innovative ways to polish your child's hidden abilities. This will help your child optimize his or her strength and use it to set appropriate lifelong goals they can set out to actualize.

For instance, if you recognize that your child is good at playing cello in school, arrange for cello classes, or hire a qualified cello instructor who can help your child refine this spark and become better at it. By doing this, you give your child an opportunity to enhance his or her inborn talent, which then becomes a skill.

Provide your child with competitive opportunities: Stay on the lookout for any relevant-to-your-child's-skill competitions or contests in your area, your child's school, or any other city. Contests give your child an opportunity to compete with other children who have similar talents and interests. This helps the child become better at what he or she loves, and identifying his or her strengths and weaknesses.

Moreover, it helps your child showcase his or her talent to the world, which gives your child the confidence to pursue his or her goals.

Give your child some breathing space: Apart from helping your child enhance his or her special spark, remember to give your child some breathing space.

When you find your child doing exceptionally well at something, you feel really happy and proud of your little one. Soon, you find yourself becoming engrossed in your child's activities.

This is a wrong approach to nurturing your child's talents. Children have a tendency of shifting from one interest to another in the growing years. If you find your child shifting to sports from music, don't be scared of letting things go. Give your child some breathing space to make his or her own decisions and try different things. Doing this helps the child gain better insight into what he or she wants.

Let them the child take the lead: Remember to let your child take the lead when it comes to choosing his or her talents, abilities, and passions. Your duty is to provide guidance, and not make decisions. Therefore, always allow your child to be in control of his or her life and interests.

Motivate your child to become better: By practicing the aforementioned tactics, you motivate your child to be better, and enhance his or her talents. Additionally, you also need to do everything in your power to increase your child's motivation over time. You can do this by rewarding your child. Make sure to reward your child with tangible and intangible elements to encourage him or her to be better at everything he or she undertakes. Praise your child when he or she achieves something, or takes a step towards realizing his or her talents. Moreover, give your child physical rewards that inspire him or her to continue working on polishing his or her talents.

Follow these strategies to assist your children recognize his or her hidden sparks, identify his or her purpose in life, and develop a growth and success mindset.

In addition to helping your child identify their talents, it is your duty as a parent to protect your child. Usually, children experience fear. It is your duty to help your child overcome, and look past this fear because fear is false evidence appearing real. In the next section, we shall examine how to help your child overcome fear.

Chapter 18: Encourage Their Interests

Naturally, since your children will all have different personalities, they will have different interests to go along with them. I roughly describe my children in the following way:

1 – The scholar
2 – The engineer
3 – The storyteller
4 – The jock
5 – The performer
6 – Too early to tell.

This may seem as though I am pigeonholing them with an arbitrary label.However, these conclusions have been reached after years of interacting, discussion and paying attention to their interests.The engineer is perhaps the clearest example of this.

For years, there did not seem to be anything he was particularly interested in.That was until he discovered a fascination with Legos.Happy that he finally had something that held his attention, my wife and I encouraged this, buying him Legos for nearly every birthday and Christmas for years.

We even took him to a Lego convention just to see what other people were doing with those little plastic bricks.Since then, his interests have shifted somewhat.Nerf guns, Minecraft, Lego robotics, and strategy games are all things that he has shown greater or lesser interest in at various points.But a common thread has been that they all involve either the building of things or carefully managing resources.

These days, he has, in classic boy fashion, developed a keen interest in things having to do with the military.

Just as important as not shutting down your kids' interests is not trying to force your own on them.This is a natural temptation for any parent, especially if there is a favorite activity that you did as a child and had to leave behind for whatever reason as you got older.

I'm not saying that you can't introduce your children to things that you are interested in.In fact, staring with what you already know and love makes perfect sense.If opera is your thing, take them to the opera.They'll never love it if they aren't exposed to it.And even if your son or daughter doesn't wind up sharing your love of the stage, they will recognize your love for it.

That in itself is important, letting your children see that there are things in this world worth loving, things that generate a sense of awe, wonder, and reverence.If they see you care about things, they will be more likely to care deeply about something themselves, even if it is not what you are moved by.

The trap I am warning against is what I call the Agassi-Woods trap.Andre Agassi is one of the best players to ever pick up a tennis racket.Watching him as I grew up was amazing and inspiring.Yet, when his biography came out, he revealed that he actually hated the game.

How can this be?He was forced to play it by his parents, who for whatever reason had determined that young Andre was going to be a tennis star.They certainly succeeded but at the cost of robbing their son of the natural joy of the sport that made his living.

Tiger Woods is another famous athlete who was raised to be a golf star practically from birth.While he has not to my knowledge expressed the same level of dislike for the game he was raised to excel at, it does not take a psychologist to speculate that his marriage issues may have been the direct result of mental problems that resulted from the constant pressure of being forced to master something that he might not have even had an interest in otherwise.

And of course books, movies, and TV shows are rife with stories of people forced into a profession by overbearing parents.Don't be that person.

On the other end of the spectrum is the parent who will try to tamp down their child's interests.Generally well meaning, the parent notices that his child has an interest in something that is relatively unusual.

It could be writing, acting, or even sports.Since success, or even just earning a decent living in these fields is quite difficult and only achieved by a relative few, the parent will tend to regard the interest as impractical or even a waste of time and try to redirect his child to something more likely to bring home enough money to live on.

Though done with the best of intentions, such an approach can rob a child of passion and ambition in anything, not just the 'impractical' desire to be an artist or dancer.Rather, allow the child to explore his interest and develop his skills. Perhaps he'll never be a household name as a video game designer but at least he will have the opportunity to find that out for himself.

Still, it is still your job as a parent to guide the child. It is important to encourage an interest, but just as important to be honest about the situation. The child should gradually be introduced to the fact that something like singing professionally takes a lot of hard work and practice.

And success will likely not come overnight if at all. This shouldn't be done to scare him away but rather as a motivator to strive to be better.

Of course, none of this will necessarily determine what he does with his life once he leaves the house. What it does mean though is that he will grow up with a healthy desire to not only ask questions about the things that pique his interest.

Even more important, by being able to explore his interests and lay them aside when he is ready, he'll have the confidence to go out and find answers to those questions and continue learning and growing as a person long after has left the four walls of your home.

Chapter 19: RELEVANCE OF DIVORCE TO CHILDREN

There are few adults and parents who are not aware of the challenges and potential difficulties that divorce imposes on children. There are literally thousands of books written about the impact of divorce on kids, both from a positive and a negative perspective. The good news out of this rather depressing research is that parents, through their actions both towards their children as well as towards each other, have a huge influence on how children will adjust to the divorce both in the short and long term.

No parent going through a divorce needs the added stress, anxiety and worry of how their actions are negatively affecting their children. By understanding how to minimize the negative aspects of divorce for children, knowing the typical responses of children to divorce, and working with the other parent to maintain the loving, nurturing environment that a child needs through the divorce, parents can help children to adjust to their new lifestyle. Stressing parent co-operation and communication with regards to raising the child or children is critical, but so is being civil, respectful and positive towards the other parent with regards to their abilities to be a wonderful Mom or Dad to the child.

Many parents struggle to help their children cope with the emotional pain of divorce and learning to live with Mom and Dad in two separate homes. Very few children, or parents for that matter, find that the time they get to spend.

together is enough. Mom and Dad working together to accommodate each other schedules and the schedules and needs of the kids will help in addressing some of the inequity that is inherent in co-parenting through a divorce and after.

Divorce is no longer an uncommon occurrence in most countries of the world. While countries in North America tend to have higher divorce rates than

other developed and developing countries, there are still some common trends and numbers to divorce around the world.

PREVALENCE OF DIVORCE

It is estimated that the overall divorce rate in the United States isapproximately 51% and in Canada it is 48%; Japan's divorce rate is about 27%, Australia is around 40% and Great Britain has a divorce rate of about 38%. The number of divorces per year tends to be increasing in many areas, with second and subsequent marriages having a higher overall divorce rate than first marriages.

As the number of divorces continues to rise in most areas and countries, so does the cultural acceptance of divorce. In the United States alone about 1.5 million children will experience divorce every year, and these are only kids that are recognized through the courts. In many cases such as step-parent divorce, the child may not be included in these numbers because they are not included in the dissolution of the marriage. Step-parent divorces can be just as problematic for the child, however, especially if they were close to the step-parent and saw them as a support person in their life.

RELATIONSHIP WITH EACH PARENT

Perhaps one of the most damaging side effects of divorce is the lack of parental involvement by one or both parents with the children through the divorce. If parents are not able to put their children's needs and emotional security in front of their own they run the risk of destroying the relationship with their kids, thereby increasing the chance that the children will have emotional and behavioral problems directly related to this damaged relationship.

It is concerning to note that:

- 40% of all children that experience a divorce do not have regular contact with their biological fathers within one year of the divorce
- Kids living with a single parent are more likely to live in poverty, more likely to be involved in gangs and criminal activities and less likely to graduate from high school or obtain a college degree
- Children that don't have a mother and father role model in their lives are more likely to engage in high risk behaviors, become sexually active much earlier, have lower self-esteem and seek attention from others rather than being satisfied with their own feelings of achievement
- 75% of all teenagers at chemical abuse treatment programs are from single parent families and report infrequent or no contact with the non-custodial parent

- According to research children of divorce that live with one parent and have no contact with the other parent are at greater risk for certain health conditions such as asthma (almost 50% higher risk), headaches, speech problems, learning difficulties, separation anxiety issues and school related behavioral problems
- Kids that have routine, constant and positive interactions with both parents on a frequent basis have the fewest health, emotional and behavioral problems
- Children with both parents involved in school progress and contact, even when they are divorced, have higher graduation rates, better grades and are less likely to drop out of school

The research is very clear. It is not so much the divorce itself that causes the stress on the children; rather it is disengagement or neglect of one or both of the parents that is damaging to children. Both parents have to work together with each other and the child to ensure that the relationship between both parents and the child remains strong throughout the separation and divorce as well as in the years to follow.

RELATIONSHIP BETWEEN SIBLINGS

During the divorce the relationship between brothers and sisters or step siblings can become damaged, just as the relationship between parents and children can be affected. Many older children are called on by parents to provide additional care for younger brothers or sisters, and this can really lead to resentment from the older kids.

Sometimes younger children may also try to assume parenting roles with younger siblings if they see Mom or Dad becoming stressed or incapable of taking on a parenting role. It is critical to keep things as normal as possible between the siblings in the family; don't ask kids to assume roles they are not ready for or roles that they resent. There is naturally going to be some tension between kids, especially if one child is very angry or upset over the divorce and is refusing to communicate or spend time with a parent. Keeping the lines of communication open, speaking positively about the kids and to the children and encouraging them to keep on being good brothers and sisters to each other is critical to maintain their relationship with each other.

CHAPTER 20: ADOLESCENT PROBLEMS

Teenagers are going to be much more aware of any problems that have been happening with the marriage dynamics. No doubt they have already been mentally bracing themselves for the announcement of separation or divorce. That doesn't mean that they have it all together when it comes to the emotional end. Teenagers are emotional and added stress and anxiety of parental relationship problems come at a very critical time in their life. Extra care and caution need to be given here to make sure they are coping well.

ANGER

You may say to yourself, "Heck, my teenager is angry all the time. What's new about that?" The type of anger I am talking about goes beyond being upset at getting in late with curfew and having to do extra chores. It is more of a "let the chair fly across the living-room" anger and can be very destructive. This level of anger is a sign of pent-up stress and should be dealt with by a professional therapist right away. A highly agitated teen can get into all kinds of trouble in school and around town.

RUNNING AWAY

Some teenagers decide that they simply won't deal with the problems and attempt or succeed at running away. Make sure you try and know all of their friends and have ways to contact them. If they do fail to come home, it might be fairly easy to find out whose house they are hanging out. Report them missing as soon as you can.

HIGH-RISK BEHAVIORS

Some teenagers will start experimenting with drugs or engaging in promiscuous activity when stress and anxiety become unbearable. The type of behavior is not uncommon for teenagers, but they are especially susceptible when separation and divorce problems strike at home. Since there is typically only one natural parent at home, they are less supervised and able to make some choices that aren't always in their best interest.

DEPRESSION AND SUICIDE

Some teenagers take the separation and divorce of parents very hard, especially if they have always felt like a close family unit. When depression strikes, you need to be very proactive. Teenagers that suddenly lose interest in their beloved hobbies, activities, become withdrawn and aloof are most likely suffering from depression. Major emotional upheaval can start them on a path of depression that can lead to thoughts or attempts of suicide. Immediate intervention needs to do.

DISCIPLINARY ISSUES AT SCHOOL

You may find that your teenager goes through a period in school in which they are spending time in detention and receiving other disciplinary actions due to fighting or talking back to authority figures. You need to make sure that these issues are being discussed with a therapist. At some levels, they will work these feelings themselves, but it could be due to residual anger and resentment they feel at the difficulties in home life. They are probably feeling a keen sense of loss at not having the absent parent around. It might help if they can spend a little extra time with the parent they do not see as often.

GETTING INTO TROUBLE WITH THE LAW

Bouts of shoplifting and other behaviors that can draw the attention of law enforcement is a big red flag that your child needs some therapy. If they have allowed stress and anger to get to a boiling point, then they could get a very much "I don't care" anymore attitude and get in all kinds of trouble. You need to intervene quickly with the help for them before they end up with a bad record or in jail. It does not mean that you bail them out of legal problems. His means you give them no choice but to do whatever the courts say AND that they HAVE to attend therapy sessions no matter what. Take the lead and be a strong parent in these situations.

Chapter 21: Changes that Occur As Your Teen Grows Up

There are a lot of different changes that your teen is going to go through while they change from being a child to an adult. Some of these changes are great for the teen and are a part of the growing up experience. But there are some changes that your teen may go through that are not considered normal. Here we will explore some of what is considered normal and some that is abnormal for the development and behavior of your teen and how you can recognize the signs of something going wrong.

Some Changes in Your Teen

First, we will take a look at some of the behavior that is considered normal in teens. Keep in mind that while it may be difficult to deal with some of these behaviors in your teen, they are normal and they show that your child is growing and maturing into the young adult they are going to be someday. Some of the normal behaviors that you can experience with your teen includes:

Extreme Emotions

There are going to be some extreme emotions that your teen will go through. Sometimes you will feel like there is a tiny little person back in your home with the tantrums and fits that are thrown. But there will be an extreme to the other side. There will also be times when the teen is excited and happy, even showing off a lot of love. These two extremes are considered normal and aren't something to worry about.

What you will need to worry about is when the teen is only experiencing the extreme lows and none of the highs. You should also worry about the child acting manic or like they can't control themselves, regardless of if there are consequences for the actions. But having little outbursts on occasion isn't something to worry too much about.

Rebellion

While rebellion in your child may be really hard to deal with, it is something that is normal when it comes to your teen. While it may make you want to pull your hair out, it is a type of experimentation that your child is going through. They are trying to see who they are as a person and what they like, or even how far they are able to push you until you go over the edge. They will get over this stage once they figure out who they want to be. You can forbid this kind of behavior, but be ready for some fighting and to impose the punishment that you promised when the rules are breached.

When you should worry occurs when your teen starts to withdraw from some longtime friends and go towards a dangerous crowd they never liked before. Extreme hyperactivity, lots of sleep, or snacking all of the time could mean that drugs are involved in the process.

Attitude

There are going to be some different attitude problems that arise with your teen. The teen is going to start to feel entitled and act in a way where they think that everyone needs to owe them something. They feel that they deserve to have new clothes, cars, time with the television, and all the latest technology. And when someone tells them that they don't get these things, they are going to overreact than ever before.

While this is a pain to deal with, you don't need to worry about this until it starts to interfere with how they are dealing with other people. If you are always fighting over whether they get something or not or other siblings are starting to fear their sibling because of the activity, you should seek some help.

There are a lot of different behaviors that are going to drive you nuts when you are dealing with your teenager, but most of these actions are considered normal. Keep a look out for something that seems a bit off or excessive since these could be signs that there is a bigger problem at hand.

Chapter 22: Getting Yourself and Your Child Ready for Changes

Before you make any changes in your life or your child's life, you have to first prepare for them. This is because change is hard on both you and your child. If you do not prepare for the changes, you will find that you will revert back to your old ways. You will also find that both you and your child will tend to fight against the changes.

The best thing that you can do is to prepare yourself, because no matter how well you prepare your child, he is going to put up a fight, at least for the first few days. There are a few steps that you can take in order to prepare yourself for the changes that you are going to make and the challenges that you are going to face.

Make a plan. As you work through this book, keep notes so that when you are finished you will be able to create a plan for yourself and your child. This plan should include what you are going to do, when you are going to do it, and how you are going to do it. For example, if your child displays a specific behavior that you know is common, what are you going to do? How will you handle it differently the next time your child displays this behavior? When do you plan on taking this action? How are you going to implement this plan to ensure that your child learns the lesson that needs to be learned, and to ensure that the child learns the skills he needs to learn in order to stop the behavior?

Think about how you would typically respond. Be honest with yourself. If your child does not pick up his toys, how do you normally respond? Do you get angry and throw the toys away, only to go out and spend more money getting a new toy because you feel guilty? Do you scream, throw things, or display other behavior that will cause the child to imitate that type of behavior?

Are you setting an example for your child? If you hit a child for hitting, you are only teaching him that it is okay for **you** to hit and not for **him** to hit; that if a person is bigger he can hit a smaller person and this is okay. Instead, change your behavior into the behavior that you want your child to display. You cannot scream all of the time and expect your child to **not** scream – you are the example and the child is going to imitate you.

Think about how the changes are going to impact your life. You have to understand that when you make changes in discipline methods, the child is going to fight and fight hard. He is going to do everything he can to break you during the first few days or weeks. You have to be prepared for this and you also need to prepare yourself for what will come after it. You have been stuck in chaos for a long time, but when all of this is over you will have peace. You will have time to take a breath and relax, but only if you stick to the plan.

The next thing that you need to think about is how the change will affect your child. In order to prepare your child for the changes that will be made, you need to sit down and explain these changes to your child, provided he's old enough to understand.

Tell him what new discipline will be used and what is expected of him.Set goals for him. For example, if the child is not used to cleaning his own bedroom and this is something that you would like for him to do, set a goal of spending ten minutes each day on cleaning. When the child reaches that goal, give him a reward. If the child does **not** reach that goal, he does not get the reward. This is part of discipline, because you are teaching him a new skill and rewarding him for doing it.

Show him what is going to happen. If you are using a chart, if you have the rules written down, or if you have set aside a time-out area, show your child these things and explain to him what they mean.

You also need to ensure that you are using effective discipline; this means that it is administered by an adult who has a bond with the child. It needs to be consistent. Before you begin any discipline routine, you need to make sure that you are going to be consistent at using it. Effective discipline depends on you even more than it depends on the child.

The extent of the discipline also has to be perceived as fair by the child. This means that not only do **you** know that the discipline you are using is not over-the-top, but the child needs to understand that as well. For example, when a child does not pick up one of his toys it would not be fair to throw away all of his toys.

The discipline has to be age-appropriate. It has to match up with the child's skills and his mental capacity. You cannot expect to discipline a three-year-old child in the same manner you would discipline a ten-year-old.

Discipline should also include guidance for the child and should be followed by a form of counseling. You need to remember that your main goal is to foster acceptable behavior and to raise a productive adult.

Chapter 23: Tantrum Management Techniques

The following is a list of tantrum management tips, tricks, and principles that you can use when an actual tantrum occurs. There are preventive measures that you can use in different situations but that will be discussed in the next chapter. The principles and ideas mentioned here will focus on what you can do when your toddler throws a fit.

Ignoring the Tantrum

Ignoring the tantrum can be considered as your first line of defense. Tantrums are heavily laced with emotions. There's just no way you can deal with that. It's your child's way of grabbing your attention fast. Remember that you are ignoring the tantrum, not your child.

Keep doing what you were previously doing but be on the lookout for your child. Be on the alert if something might break or injure your tot.

Time for a Time Out

Find a safe place where you can put your toddler. If you have a younger tot (ages 1 to 2) then you can put him/her in the crib and wait for them to calm down. If you're dealing with an older toddler (ages 2 and above) then you can find a chair or some other safe place where they can let it all out. Make sure that there isn't anything within their reach that they can throw or topple over – you don't want them to hurt themselves.

Time outs allow your tots to vent their frustrations. Remember that they just don't know how to pull it together. You always have the option to leave them there or stay there and hold them as they vent. But remember not to talk to them.

Once the time out moment is over you should come over and talk to your child. Talk about what happened. You should also set your expectations that you don't like them shouting, stomping, and others.

You may have to repeat these sessions several times.

Misdirection

This is not just a magic trick – it's an anti-tantrum trick too! Whenever you see your child starts to throw a fit (i.e. the full blown thing is just starting to erupt) then you can take away your child's attention from that thing that was just irritating or frustrating them and direct their attention to something else.

You can use something funny; show them a colorful toy or picture, or offer a snack if you think that your child may be hungry. Some parents have a full bag of treats, toys, and other interesting stuff to take their kid's mind off of the tantrum. Sometimes all you need to do is to bring your child to another location – take him away from that place or thing that was frustrating him.

Give Them a Different Option

Someone once said that teaching discipline is more than just telling someone to stop a certain behavior. It is more like teaching someone a better behavior – give them a different choice. You can talk to your older toddlers and tell them that if they are angry, instead of biting, throwing stuff, stomping their feet, or shouting, they can just say they are angry. You can also promise them that if they say that they got angry or upset that you will give your full attention to them. Remember to follow through on that promise!

Make It Fun

This is also another type of misdirection. This tantrum management tactic works better for younger kids. If they start to cry or throw a fit then show them something fun or tasty. You can show them a funny picture or toy. Show them a snack that you want to give them. It will take their mind off the thing that was frustrating them.

However, before you begin the game, give the treat, or before you allow them to play the toy, make sure to affirm the fact that they are behaving nicely. Don't give the treat etc. when they're still crying or being angry or else you're giving the wrong message. The reward (i.e. the fun thing) should only come within reach if they stop throwing a tantrum.

Chapter 24: The Affects for Parents

There are endless reasons as to why being a single parent is a bad idea and most of these reasons are statistics about the children involved.Those statistics are real, and the evidence of the effects on the children is undeniable.Through single parent households, we are raising up children that are insecure, vulnerable, struggle with inability to socialize, behavioral issues, and so much more.And if a parent has more than one child they are trying to raise, chances are, they will experience some serious issues in at least one of them.

But what about the parents and their life as a single parent?As if knowing the affects on children and teens is not enough for parents, what about what life as a single parent does to them?A single parent of divorce often trades one set of problems and issues for another.Many single parents venture into being a single parent out of personal desire, and others are forced into that lifestyle.Whatever the reasoning behind the single parent household, everyone involved suffers, especially the kids, but also the parent.

Single parents are forced to wear many hats and living up to the title that each hat bears is nearly impossible.Single parents often deal with the guilt of a divorce or inability to provide for their children the way other parents can provide.Sometimes the guilt and burden are overwhelming and many parents feel they are prisoners to their shame.Many times those overwhelming emotions put distance between the child and the parent because the parent withdraws emotionally – which of course has damning effects on both the parent and the child.

Single parents almost never have time for themselves.Their lives are consumed by their children and the daily lives of their children.This can bring unwanted frustration and bitterness towards the situation and often manifest itself on the kids.Homes where there are two parents do not experience this dynamic as often because the parents can support each other.Unfortunately for single parents, there is no down time or alone time.

While in households where there are two parents, a mother or father can choose to spend time with friends outside the home and know that their child or children are properly being cared for by the other parent.However, in single parent households, those privileges do not always exist.The single parent may be deserving of a night out, but may not be a good idea, especially if your child has been in daycare all week.In addition, finances are typically limited in single parent households as well.

There is not a lot of emotional support for single parents and not a lot of time for single parents to get support.Single parents will often seek emotional support or companionship through the opposite sex, and when that happens, there are always issues involved.Because the kids need to be the top priority dating should be very limited but unfortunately, many single parents are so in need of the support that they entertain relationships that are damaging to them, and their children.

There are many reasons why single parenting is a bad idea and mainly the negative affects on the children, however, the parents involved need to take a look at what they will go through as well.Perhaps they may re-thing their decision.

Chapter 25: How to Be in the Dating Game As a Single Parent

You Have To Make Time

This is probably the most important of all rules. YOU, yes you, HAVE to make time. Unless you want to stay single the rest of your life, this is a requirement. Of course, if you are single, you probably wouldn't be reading this chapter. Just like with anything in life, you can't make excuses. If we really want to do something, we'll make time.

We'll do tricks up and down, use resources from A to Z to make something happen. If it doesn't require you to be out all night, sparks can fly (or fizz) in just a few hours for a dinner, movie, etc. You get the picture. But, you say, 'I don't have a baby sitter or child care'. Well, not yet, you don't. You've got to get creative if you're going to get the chance to date and take care of you.

The easiest route to take is ask family. If you have a family member who has children, then offer to exchange babysitting time. Nothing big, like I said, a few hours, and adding another kid into your plate of things as the return favor can be as simple as just letting them watch a movie or playing games.

Think simple, we're single parents, remember, we don't need to use energy in places we don't need to. Another route is to ask another parent to watch your child. Yes, another parent, but you say, I don't want to ask.

You'd be surprised how many of your friends will help you, most parents already know it's hard to parent with both parents, let alone half the duo. My married friends always loved the possibility that I may meet someone and fall in love, and you know the rest of that fairy tale.

They loved the idea so much they'd watch my kid. I even had one friend kick me out of the house and told me not to come back till tomorrow. Of course you can't abuse their generosity, but you can also to offer to take their kids with you to the movies or the park, somewhere the kids can run wild. And you the parent, can sit there like the vegetable you sometimes deserve to be!

Yes, there are more possibilities, there are single parent groups out there that exist for parents to help each other. No doubt there are parents in those groups who are in a similar situation. If there's not already a babysitting exchange group, try to get one started.

If that is too much for you to take on, find a parent who has similar parenting characteristics as you do and see if you can work out a schedule to watch each other's kids. Just like they recommend married couples go out at least once a week, I think the same goes for single parents.

One date a week, not a great number, but one is better than none. None won't get you in the dating game! I caution you when meeting another parent that you get to know them well before you do this babysitting exchange, not to be the negative person, but you never really know what people are capable of. Several play dates or dinners at the nearby restaurant, where it's a free dinner for kids, would work.

Okay, you're shy, you live far, you live in a small town, for whatever reason, the single parent group isn't an option or any of the other ones listed before, what now? Well, there's the baby sitter route. Yes, it's expensive, but if you look around for a baby sitter with a low rate (possibly a teenage kid) and go for just a few hours, it can be doable.

It'll be an expense, but should you meet the person of your dreams, it'll pay dividends. Just like the baby sitting exchange group, you should also take time to get to know the person that is watching your kid.

Recommendations from friends is a good place to start. Then with the names you have, you can interview different folks after you've put together your list of care bouts. You can also do a test run to see how they interact with the kid.

It's also good to keep a list of a few baby sitters, especially if they're teenagers, they tend to get the busiest (which is a good thing). Another option to cut cost is to share the babysitter with another parent, you just have to decide and agree to whose house you'll leave the kids at.

If all else fails, and you have no other options, provided you at least trust the person enough to let them in your house, you can wait until the kids are asleep and have a casual time to hang out--play video games, board games, talk, the possibilities are endless.

You Have To Take That Spit Bib Off

Before you go running out the door with your baby sitting situation lined up, you need come right. Step in front of the mirror, and very objectively look at what you see. Yes, spit up here and there, a bib on this shoulder, maybe you're still in your pajamas.

That isn't going to work in the dating world. I know it's comfortable, I get it, who doesn't want to be comfortable. But if comfortable is what got our dating world going, then throw out the fashion and let's live pajama style! Sadly, no, we have to spend effort to get ready and be at our best.

Get rid of the baby evidence or kid painting or chalk, whatever it may be, it needs to go. Don't worry, you can always return to it.

Don't be afraid to hand over the responsibilities to whomever is taking care of your child, provided you did your homework on child care and you have friends you can trust, you should be at ease knowing your child is in good hands.

Should anything arise, a cell phone number on both ends will suffice. I like to get a new outfit for a new date, but that's just me. I feel good when I have new threads and I can always have a different look, it gives me confidence. Single parent budgets don't always allow for purchases like that, so you can just go into your closet and choose the most appropriate and flattering outfit.

I'll leave it at that, my fashion guru degree hasn't arrived yet, so, I trust that you can decide for yourself what you look good in. Just make sure if you're going somewhere fancy, you dress fancy. Likewise, if you're going somewhere casual, pick out the most flattering casual outfit you can.

If you're a woman, make sure it accentuates your curves without being overly revealing (unless you're going for something besides 'dating'), a guy wants to know he's going out on a date with a girl. And guys, try to leave the sneakers that don't tie, at home.

We're grown folks here, and there's always time later to let your inner kid be.

Until then, keep your man face on. Best foot forward, that's what you have to go by. And sadly, first impressions mean a lot, so the more polished you are, the better chances you have to get through the date and possibly onto others.

Confidence

Okay, got the baby sitter, the right outfit, there's still a few more things you can do. I know the single parent lifestyle really sucks, I know there's times when you just feel like you want to quit and that you're going to break. There's been lots of days when I just thought I had nothing left to give.

It's a hard life, I would never take away from that. It is tough, it pulls strength out of you that you never knew you had. Maybe, at times, you wake up, wishing you had some sort of relief or at least someone to support and be confident in you. Again, as single parents, we don't have that. We have to find it in ourselves or at least find friends who will listen to our gripes. Dates are not the place to do that. NOBODY wants a complainer.

On the other token, it's a warning sign if the person you're on a date with or dating doesn't seem to be interested in the things you have to say about your child. Your child is a part of you, if they can't like (love, eventually) them, it's time to reevaluate.

Whatever doubt, confusion, and difficulties you face with single parenting, save those for you and your friends. Eventually if the person becomes your mate, then by all means, bombs away. Until then, try to pick your head up, think about all the positive things you do have as a single parent and just a human being.

Single parent may be your parenting status, but it doesn't have to define who we are as a whole. That is just part of the picture of who we are, there's our background, our goals, our dreams, our career, our hobbies, our faith, our talents, the list goes on. We ALL have those, constantly being aware of those good parts of us can keep us with our head up.

I remember for the longest time, I felt shame for being a single parent. No one ever really plans to be a single parent, but it happens. I knew there were dating sites where the guys didn't want to date me because I had a child. I know that my dating pool shrunk after I had my son.

Guys that were interested in me in college and after lost interest and only wanted friendship. But I had to tell myself a few things. First, I had to tell myself that I wouldn't want to be with someone who couldn't accept my child, they didn't deserve to be in either or our lives.

Second, I had to constantly remind myself that I had a son whom I loved beyond anything and if it had to be that I was a single parent as my life, so be it. I would tell myself that over and over until I really started believing it. Third, finding a partner as a single parent isn't an impossible feat.

Many have done it before you and more than likely you can even pick out friends that have found someone. With that, you should be proud of who are you, from beginning to end, head to toe, and all the way around.

You have you and that's all you have. If you're not having you, then people see that and will treat you likewise. And when you take off on this date, don't forget to smile, again, you have much to be thankful for, people like happy people. Nobody wants to be with someone who's just unhappy.

Hope

No matter what, single parents should always have hope. Our lives may not be the way we planned it and times are tough. There were times I didn't know how I'd provide for my son, but there is always a way.

The human spirit is strong, as long as we have hope. The moment we lose hope, what else is there to look forward to?

Something's got to keep us going through the days, otherwise everyday will be a chore and everyday will look just like the last.

I use prayer in my life and it wasn't up until recently that I started using it in my dating life. It's helped me both get through the days as a single parent, but it also helped me to have patience in my dating life.

Maybe, you like affirmations, then find a great source or a great book, and know that you are value just simply as your existence, no matter what life circumstances you are dealt. We don't live in a perfect world and even married couples have their struggles, it's all a part of life. But we do have to embrace it.

If you truly believe there is someone out there for you or that you want a partner, then keep it going. It's a lot of work, but so is anything in life. The more comfortable and confident you are with yourself, the more it shows and people know that.

I know that for me, once I stopped looking and I was at my highest confidence, the men came running. Confidence is sexy and attracts people alike. And the more you reaffirm yourself, have hope, and confidence, the more you'll just feel better in general.

Some may not even need a mate. There is that possibility, but you never know. And until you get yourself out there, you'll always wonder.

Chapter 26: Communication with Your Child

Do you remember when you were younger and sitting on the fringes of a discussion by the adults in your family? Do you remember how badly you wanted to add your opinion—to contribute to the conversation? The adults were interested in adult opinion and ignored you. There is an old adage that says that children should be seen and not heard. This was based on the general expectation that youthful opinion carried little importance and respect should be paid to the elders.

At the same time we want to maintain communication with our youngsters. We want to know everything that's going on in their lives—generally so we can monitor their safety and exposure. Our world is considerably different from that of our parents'. We are living in a global environment, subject to societal influences that are not subject to our government or laws. Our children are exposed to ideas, rebellions, religions, political views, sexual deviations and theoretical concepts that fall outside those we introduce into their home life and upbringing. As parents we have lost control of many of the values and ethics we would have our children respect. Innocence is shattered at a far earlier age than ever known before.

How do we cope with this? How do we protect and filter our childrens' exposures? The truth is that unless we create a private bubble where we assume the role of judge, educator and religious guidance, we probably cannot. The best we may be able to hope for is to be aware of what they are learning.

For this reason, communication with our children is all the more important. And since they are being exposed to the world at such an early age now, there is no time like the present to becoming involved.

The first decision is to determine when we should simply be "aware" and when it's necessary for us to become involved. How do we tune in to our childrens' radio stations without them tuning us out in return?

As our own worlds become more and more transparent we understand the need for privacy. Each of us needs to feel that we can operate with autonomy, in at least some aspect of our lives. Our own values are clouded. Is it permissible for a website like Facebook to sell our personal preferences to retail marketers and list our names in the Google search engine? Is it reasonable that our employer have access to our private communications with our friends and family? Where does the right to privacy begin?

It begins at home. The ethics we utilize in our homes with our children will set the precedents for the coming generations. We are at this point caught between a generation who instilled the right to privacy as one of our basic freedoms; and the demands of rebellious, anti-establishment maverick computer programmers who lure us into convenient communication with a total lack of respect for what we share in a supposedly private environment. In short, we were brought up better than those who hold our futures in their hands.

So, when it comes down to communicating with our children, we need to understand their expectations and values. Elementary-aged children today believe that transparency is simply the way it is done. They expose not only their own privacy, but yours. Besides the obvious opportunity for this information to be exploited by the wrong people, it is downright dangerous.

Therefore, we need to know how to communicate, and at a level our children understand.

The first way to accomplish this is to simply listen and observe. Children are curiously honest when treated with consideration. While they may not respond to direct questions such as, "What do you and Bobby talk about when you text?" they may respond to another approach. "What do you think is more important? Being the first to try something out or waiting until your friends go first and fitting in?" These sorts of conversations can be very telling. They reveal your child's mindset and auto-response; that's the same sort of reaction they will have when faced with sticky situations such as pre-marital sex or drug use. You can determine their character and personal ethics.

What better way to learn about a person than to sit down to a board game on a Sunday night with a bowl of popcorn and some laughter? What makes your child frustrated? What sort of humor do they enjoy? Are they loyal or opportunistic? Do they break the rules of the game openly or behave in a sneakier, less conspicuous manner? How do they treat you? Do they give mom a hard time or do they respectfully defer to her enjoyment?

Rather than cataloging words, these sorts of activities give you a legend that predicts how your child will respond to many different scenarios in their life. You will learn whether they are trustworthy, subject to peer pressure, confident, experimental, or whether they are thrill-seekers. Sit nearby when they play video games and study their tendencies. Are they aggressive or defensive? Do they choose alter egos who are violent or protective? Do they break rules and how do they respond to losing the game? There is so much here to observe.

Learn to trust when it is deserved. To do otherwise is to undermine their effort to grow as individuals.

Conclusion

Parenting is an important aspect of our life and needs much attention than any other issues in one's life. Parenting involves many aspects of life like education, morality, ethics, discipline, and training to make children successful in their life. Definition of a good person can vary depending on the fact that who is being asked. Defining a good parent is however same as trying to define a good person. However, some generalizations are there that are common of a good parent. Parents should have a basic love of really caring about their children. This involves paying attention and showing affection to the child. A good family atmosphere should be created and maintained by parents. . "A good parent should also be a good person". They should possess the capital and resources to support the baby for years as their birth is only a smaller part of all this. "A good parent should also be a good person". A crucial role in child development is played by parenting styles. In fact, research has uncovered that parenting styles can impact a youngster's mental, intellectual, and social development, influencing the child both in early years and as a grown-up. There are four commonly known parenting styles including, authoritative, authoritarian, permissive, and uninvolved parenting. This report has also addressed the parental rights and obligation, parental philosophy and factors affecting the philosophy of parenting.

www.ingramcontent.com/pod-product-compliance
Lightning Source LLC
Chambersburg PA
CBHW072015070526
44583CB00015B/1487